THE
NEW
WAY
TO
CAKE

BENJAMINA EBUEHI

as seen on
The Great British Bake Off

THE
NEW
WAY
TO
CAKE

SIMPLE RECIPES WITH
EXCEPTIONAL FLAVOR

PAGE STREET
PUBLISHING CO.

PAGE STREET
PUBLISHING CO.

Copyright © 2019 Benjamina Ebuehi

First published in 2019 by
Page Street Publishing Co.
27 Congress Street, Suite 105
Salem, MA 01970
www.pagestreetpublishing.com

Distributed by Macmillan, sales in Canada by The Canadian Manda Group.

23 22 21 20 19   1 2 3 4 5

ISBN-13: 978-1-62414-867-5
ISBN-10: 1-62414-867-0

Library of Congress Control Number: 2019937729

Cover and book design by Kylie Alexander for Page Street Publishing Co.
Photography by Holly Wulff Petersen

Printed and bound in China

TO EVERYONE WHO
SIMPLY LOVES CAKE

CONTENTS

INTRODUCTION

You can't go wrong with cake. There's nothing quite like generously slicing up a homemade cake to the delight of friends and family eager to dig in . . . the soft crumb gladly giving way under the weight of the knife and the filling spilling out of the sides. It's truly one of life's delights. A wedge of chocolate cake after a frantic day can bring much comfort, while turning up at a friend's door with cake in hand—just because—can convey such a deeply personal connection.

I come from a family full of wonderful cooks who make the most vibrant, expressive and comforting dishes. Growing up in London in a Nigerian household meant big, bold flavors and plenty of chili, spices, stews, yams and plantains. As much as the cooking and savory side were great, the sweeter side of things was pretty much nonexistent. When it came to having dessert after a meal, aside from a sturdy apple crumble or a humble rice pudding, I had to fill in the gaps myself and started experimenting in the kitchen with a children's baking book bought by my mum.

It didn't take long for me to become completely enthralled with the magic of baking: the way that eggs and sugar puffed and rose majestically just by whisking or how a chocolatey pool of batter came out of the oven after what seemed like an age, tall, fudgy and infinitely better than the sum of its parts. I knew that this was a world I wanted to be immersed in. Quickly working my way through other baking books, it was always the chapters on cakes that attracted me the most, and I sought to create cakes with my own style of modern, creative flavors. Growing up in the cultural melting pot of London meant that I had easy access to the most vibrant ingredients and tastes from all over the world— whether that was tahini or sumac from the Middle East, West African plantains or tropical passionfruit and mangoes. These all heavily influenced my baking style, which focuses on showing off the ingredients and putting the flavors at the forefront without overshadowing them with excessive decoration. I firmly believe that decoration should complement without overshadowing! There's been a noticeable shift toward a more minimal, stripped-back approach to decoration within the baking world. Home bakers want simple cakes that stand out with new, unexpected flavors, and this book is full of exactly that.

Fast forward a few years and I find myself on a little show called *The Great British Bake Off*. I had watched it religiously for years, constantly in awe and impressed by all those people brave enough to bake in that tent. I look back at that time as one of intense recipe development, endless baking, early starts for filming, numerous trains back and forth, hours spent in supermarkets buying up all the butter in London, tears when I couldn't get something to work right after the millionth attempt and the countless prayers asking for the strength to just keep going. On the show, I grew so much as a baker, both in confidence and creativity. Having to constantly come up with ideas for breads, pastries and everything in between pushed me to be bold enough to try new combinations and again, it was the cakes that brought me the most joy.

Cake week was the very first week, and I remember baking a white chocolate and salted praline cake that I had practiced numerous times. Halfway through making the Swiss meringue buttercream, I completely panicked because it wouldn't come together the way it was supposed to. Turns out, all it needed was a bit more time to whip up, and it came out beautifully. From that experience I learned to just trust my baking instincts, be patient with the process and keep calm in the kitchen. The more you bake and practice, the more these instincts will develop and you'll be able to avoid breaking down over a cake! Wild as it was, it was such a sweet time (in more ways than one), and every time I think about it, I can't help but smile at how much I learned in such a short space of time as well as how fortunate I was to meet eleven new friends who love baking just as much as I do.

The New Way to Cake is all about exploring ingredients, textures, flavors and combinations in a way that you haven't before. I want us to go beyond the cakes we usually turn to and bring forward something a little more unexpected. By incorporating unanticipated ingredients such as sumac, plantains and pomegranate molasses, which are all incredible in their own right, we unravel and enjoy them in new ways and create fresh, modern bakes. I've stripped back the styling to let the cakes and the parts that make them really shine. We're not hiding things under thick layers of laborious fondant but rather allowing them to look effortless and inviting.

Beautiful, even in the cracks and mishaps, cakes are one of my favorite things, and I am so excited to share the recipes in this book with you. This book is for everyone who wants their cakes to have both style and substance. I hope that you are inspired to create something new, expand your cake repertoire and come across recipes that you want to return to again and again. When in doubt, choose cake.

Benjamina

TIPS FOR BAKING CAKES AT HOME

I want you to get the best out of this book and produce cakes at home that come out great every time. In order to do that, there are a few important notes to bear in mind before starting:

MEASUREMENTS   When it comes to baking, precision is key. For my U.S. readers, I strongly recommend investing in a digital scale in order to get the best results. Grams are the most accurate way to measure, giving you consistent bakes every time. Cups can be notoriously inaccurate, resulting in cakes that don't come out the way they were intended to, and this can be frustrating. (I've included both gram and cup measurements in these recipes.) For ingredients measured in teaspoons and tablespoons, be sure to use actual measuring spoons for accuracy.

TEMPERATURE   The temperature of your ingredients also plays an important role in baking. Things such as butter, eggs, milk and yogurt should always be at room temperature before using, unless the temperature is stated otherwise in the recipe. This is so the ingredients can trap in more air, which helps avoid a curdled batter. All eggs used are medium in the U.K. and large in the United States. Milk is always full fat unless stated differently.

Baking at the right temperature greatly affects the quality of your cakes, and home ovens can vary immensely in their accuracy. It may be worth investing in an oven thermometer to make sure your oven is properly calibrated. As a general rule, if you're using a fan oven, be sure to lower the stated temperature by 70°F (20°C), as these ovens tend to cook things faster.

SUGAR   When it comes to sugar, most of the recipes will use superfine sugar (called caster sugar in the U.K.), which is finer than granulated sugar but not as fine as powdered/icing sugar. Superfine sugar is usually preferable in cakes as it dissolves quickly when beating with butter or making a meringue. If you can't get ahold of this, you can substitute with granulated sugar, but you may want to grind it very briefly in a food processor to break down the granules. Just be careful not to overdo it, as you'll end up with powdered sugar if you grind it for too long. Your processed sugar should feel like coarse sand.

EQUIPMENT   Be sure to check which size pan the cake will be baked in before starting the recipe. If you need to use a different size, you'll have to adjust the cooking time. Generally, using a pan larger than the recipe states will require a shorter cooking time, while using a smaller pan will require a longer time in the oven.

Always grease your baking pans with butter or cooking spray, even if the pan is nonstick. I also always line the bottom and sides of my pans with parchment paper for easy removal.

For the layer cake recipes, there are a couple of pieces of equipment that will help make decorating much easier. A cake turntable and a plastic or metal bench scraper both allow you to achieve perfectly layered cakes with smooth buttercream edges in no time.

NUTS & CARAMEL

Watching simple white sugar bubble up and caramelize into liquid gold is a thing of beauty. Swirl in a generous pinch of flaky sea salt, and you've got yourself the best sauce for dipping, drizzling or just eating straight from the jar. While plain caramel works well in most situations, there are so many possibilities to introduce new flavors. It could be a swirl of tahini in my Hazelnut & Tahini Caramel Cake (page 28) or some unexpected fresh sage leaves in my Apple Cake with Sage Caramel (page 14).

Caramel can be tricky to get right and may take a couple of tries before you get the hang of it. But once you've mastered it, you'll be able to whip up a quick batch of caramel sauce for your cakes in no time. Do be careful when heating the sugar for caramel; this process will require all of your attention, as it can burn quite quickly. And as mesmerizing as golden, bubbling sugar looks in the pan, the temperature will be significantly hotter than boiling water so don't be tempted to stick your finger in the pan. I tell you this from experience! If you're a little nervous, you could wear a pair of oven mitts to protect your hands from splashes of hot sugar.

One of caramel's best partners is nuts. From pecans to hazelnuts, walnuts and almonds, quite a few of the cakes in this chapter combine both to create sweet-and-salty pairings that I know are loved by many. I bake with ground almonds quite a fair bit and love the texture that they bring as well as their moisture from the natural oils. The Almond & Amaretto Cake (page 23) is a real delight—a double hit of almond flavor held together by a dense yolk-rich batter. The Peanut Butter Banana Bread (page 27) is an updated classic made all the more beautiful with the sliced bananas laying on top. All the recipes here bring a comforting stickiness and nuttiness, and are incredibly scrumptious—sweet yet sophisticated.

APPLE CAKE WITH SAGE CARAMEL

FOR THE CRISPS
1 apple of your choice (I used Braeburn)

FOR THE CAKE

2 apples of your choice (I used Braeburn)

¼ cup (60 ml) water

2 eggs

⅔ cup (150 g) light brown sugar

½ cup (120 ml) vegetable oil

1 tsp vanilla bean paste

1⅓ cups (175 g) all-purpose flour

1½ tsp (8 g) baking powder

½ tsp baking soda

1 tsp ground cinnamon

This cake couldn't be more autumnal if it tried. The curled apple crisps mimic fallen leaves while the soft cake makes use of the abundance of the season's bounty. What really brings this all together, though, is the sage caramel. Earthy and fragrant, it's not a common herb used in sweet recipes, but it is such an unexpected delight. I adore both the smell and taste of sage, so I use quite a few leaves in the caramel. You can always adjust it to taste.

YIELD: 1 SQUARE 8 X 8-INCH (20 X 20-CM) CAKE

Preheat the oven to 285°F (140°C). Line a baking tray with parchment paper.

To make the crisps, take 1 apple and, starting from the bottom, slice it thinly through the core. Use a mandoline, if you have one, to get even slices or use a very sharp knife. Place the apple slices on the baking tray, making sure not to overlap them. Bake for 45 to 55 minutes, turning them over once, or until they're dry to the touch and begin to curl up. Thicker slices will take longer to crisp, so keep an eye on them to make sure they don't brown too much. Transfer the crisps to a wire rack to cool completely.

Increase the oven temperature to 350°F (180°C). Grease an 8 x 8-inch (20 x 20-cm) cake pan and line the bottom with parchment paper.

To make the cake, peel, core and roughly chop the apples, and place them in a small saucepan with the water. Cook over a low heat for 8 to 10 minutes, or until the apples have softened. Remove from the heat and mash them lightly with a fork to make applesauce. It's fine to have a few chunks. Set aside.

Using a stand mixer or electric whisk, whisk together the eggs and sugar for 2 to 3 minutes, or until the eggs are pale and thick. With the mixer still running, slowly pour in the oil and continue to beat for another minute. Stir in the applesauce, vanilla, flour, baking powder, baking soda and cinnamon. Pour the batter into the prepared pan and bake for 35 to 40 minutes, or until the cake is well browned and is springy to the touch. Remove from the oven and let it cool completely in the pan.

(Continued)

APPLE CAKE WITH SAGE CARAMEL (CONTINUED)

½ cup (120 ml) heavy cream

8–10 fresh sage leaves, plus extra to decorate

1 cup (200 g) granulated sugar

¼ tsp flaky sea salt

FOR THE FROSTING

¼ cup (50 g) unsalted butter

⅓ cup (50 g) confectioners' sugar

¾ cup (180 g) cream cheese

A handful of roughly chopped walnuts

To make the sage caramel, add the cream and sage to a small saucepan. Bring the cream to a simmer, and then remove from the heat, cover and let it steep and cool for 20 minutes. Once cool, discard the sage leaves.

In a separate saucepan, heat the sugar over a medium heat until it dissolves and turns a light amber color. Swirl the pan every now and again to help the sugar caramelize evenly. Once it reaches a golden amber color, slowly pour in the cream. Be careful, as the caramel will bubble up rapidly. Whisk constantly and let the caramel simmer for 30 seconds before removing from the heat and stirring in the salt. Pour it into a bowl to cool.

To make the frosting, beat the butter and sugar with an electric whisk until the mixture is pale and creamy. Add the cream cheese and beat for 1 minute, or until smooth. Beat in 3 tablespoons (60 g) of the sage caramel and set aside until you're ready to decorate.

When the cake is completely cool, remove it from the pan and place it on a cake stand or serving plate. Spoon on the frosting, spreading it evenly and leaving about a ½ inch (1 cm) free around the edges. Drizzle on the remaining sage caramel and then place the apple crisps, sage leaves and walnuts on top.

MAPLE–WALNUT LAYER CAKE

FOR THE MAPLE PASTRY CREAM

1 cup (240 ml) milk

1 tsp vanilla

4 egg yolks

¼ cup (50 g) superfine/caster sugar

2½ tbsp (38 ml) maple syrup

4 tsp (10 g) all-purpose flour

1 tbsp (8 g) cornstarch

1 tbsp (15 g) unsalted butter

½ cup (120 ml) heavy cream

FOR THE CAKE

2¾ cups (340 g) all-purpose flour

1 tbsp (15 g) baking powder

1½ cups (340 g) unsalted butter

1⅔ cups (340 g) superfine/caster sugar

6 eggs

2 tsp (10 ml) vanilla

½ cup (120 ml) milk

1⅓ cups (160 g) finely chopped walnuts

Confectioners' sugar, to dust

Whole walnuts, to decorate

I spent about a year living in Canada while getting my undergraduate degree, and one of the things I couldn't get enough of was the maple syrup. I didn't realize that I'd been enjoying such an inferior version back in the U.K., so I promptly stocked up before heading home. With a woodier flavor compared to honey, I find that it pairs really well with the earthy walnuts that speckle the sponge layers in this recipe. The maple pastry cream, rich and custardy, makes a welcome change from the usual sweeter buttercream.

YIELD: 1 ROUND 8-INCH (20-CM) LAYER CAKE

Preheat the oven to 350°F (180°C). Grease four round 8-inch (20-cm) cake pans and line with parchment paper.

To make the pastry cream, add the milk and vanilla to a medium-size saucepan and bring to a simmer. Remove from the heat and set aside. In a medium bowl, whisk together the eggs, sugar and maple syrup until the sugar dissolves and the eggs become pale. Add the flour and cornstarch and whisk to get a thick paste. Pour a ladle of the warm milk into the eggs, whisking constantly. This helps to temper the eggs so they don't scramble. Continue to ladle in the warm milk while whisking, and then pour the egg mix back into the saucepan.

Heat the custard base over medium heat while whisking constantly. The custard will start to thicken after 1 to 2 minutes. Once it's smooth and thick enough to coat the back of a spoon, remove it from the heat and stir in the butter until it's fully melted. Transfer the custard to a clean bowl and cover with plastic wrap, making sure the wrap touches the surface of the custard. This stops a skin from forming. Let it cool to room temperature before chilling in the fridge for at least 2 hours.

To make the cake, sift together the flour and baking powder in a large bowl and set aside. Using a stand mixer or electric whisk, beat the butter and superfine sugar for 3 to 5 minutes, or until pale and fluffy. Add the eggs, one at a time, beating well after each addition. If the mixture starts to curdle, add a tablespoon (8 g) of the flour mix. In a small bowl, stir the vanilla into the milk and set aside. Add half of the flour to the butter mixture and beat on low speed until combined. Pour in the milk, followed by the remaining flour. Mix until smooth, and then stir in the chopped walnuts. Divide the batter evenly among the cake pans and bake for 20 to 25 minutes, or until the cakes are golden brown and a toothpick inserted comes out clean. Let the cakes cool for 10 minutes before removing them from the pans and transferring to a wire rack to cool completely.

(Continued)

MAPLE-WALNUT LAYER CAKE (CONTINUED)

To assemble the cake, take the pastry cream out of the fridge and give it a good whisk to break up any lumps and make it smooth. In a separate bowl, whip the heavy cream until you have stiff peaks and fold this into the pastry cream.

If any of the cake layers are uneven, level them with a sharp, serrated knife or cake leveler. Place one layer on a cake board or cake stand. Spoon or pipe on a layer of pastry cream and repeat with the next two cake layers. When you get to the fourth cake, place this topside down so you have a completely flat top. Dust with confectioners' sugar and sprinkle the extra walnuts on top.

Tip: If you don't have four cake pans, you can bake the cake in two deep pans and increase the baking time 10 to 15 minutes or until a toothpick comes out clean. Then slice each cake in half once baked.

CARAMELIZED PLANTAIN UPSIDE-DOWN CAKE

FOR THE TOPPING

¼ cup (60 g) unsalted butter

½ cup plus 1 tbsp (120 g) light muscovado sugar

Pinch of flaky sea salt, as desired

1 tbsp (15 ml) dark rum

2–3 ripe plantains

FOR THE CAKE

1⅓ cups (175 g) all-purpose flour

1 tsp baking powder

½ tsp baking soda

¼ tsp salt

1 tsp ground cinnamon

½ cup (115 g) unsalted butter, softened

¾ cup plus 2 tbsp (180 g) superfine/caster sugar

2 eggs

Scant ⅔ cup (150 ml) plain yogurt, divided

Ice cream, for serving (optional)

Plantains are the food of my childhood. If you grew up in an African or Caribbean household, you know that the smell of sweet fried plantains wafting through the house was enough to make you do a happy dance. While traditionally eaten as part of a savory meal, when ripe enough, underneath that black mottled skin lies a sweetness that lends itself beautifully to desserts such as this.

YIELD: 1 ROUND 9-INCH (23-CM) CAKE

Preheat the oven to 350°F (180°C). Grease the bottom and sides of a round 9-inch (23-cm) cake pan and line the bottom with parchment paper.

To make the topping, add the butter and muscovado sugar to a small saucepan and cook over medium heat for 2 to 3 minutes, stirring until the sugar is dissolved. Remove from the heat and stir in the salt and rum. Pour the caramel into the cake pan and spread it evenly across the base. Slice the plantains into thirds lengthwise and arrange them on top of the caramel. Try not to overlap them—it's okay if not all the caramel is covered by the plantains.

To make the cake, sift together the flour, baking powder, baking soda, salt and cinnamon in a large bowl and set aside.

Using a stand mixer or electric whisk, beat the butter and sugar together until pale and creamy. Add the eggs one at a time, beating well after each addition. If the mixture looks like it's curdled, stir in a tablespoon (8 g) of the flour mix. Add one-third of the flour while mixing on low speed. Pour in half of the yogurt, followed by another third of flour. Repeat with the remaining yogurt and finally, the remaining flour. Pour the batter on top of the plantains, spreading it into an even layer. Bake for 35 to 45 minutes, or until a toothpick inserted into the center comes out clean. If there's just caramel on the toothpick, you're good to go!

Let the cake cool in the pan for 10 minutes before running a palette knife around the edge of the cake. Turn the cake upside down onto a plate or cake stand. If any caramel is still in the pan, spoon it back on top. This cake is best served warm on the day it's made with a scoop of ice cream.

ALMOND & AMARETTO CAKE

1¼ cups (250 g) superfine/caster sugar

½ cup (120 ml) water

1 tsp vanilla extract

2 cups (200 g) ground almonds

3 tbsp (45 g) salted butter

8 egg yolks

1 egg

3 tbsp (45 ml) amaretto

Confectioners' sugar, as desired

I grew up in Vauxhall, South London, which was an area with a large Portuguese community full of traditional restaurants and bakeries. This cake is inspired by the Portuguese cake Toucinho do Ceu and the texture is quite unique; the sheer number of egg yolks used provides an almost custard-like feel contrasted against the ground almonds, which is the only thing holding it all together. This makes the cake both naturally gluten free and perfectly moist. I've gone for a double hit of almonds with a good measure of amaretto for a warm kick.

I will point out that this cake is quite sweet, so only a sliver is needed alongside a double espresso.

YIELD: 1 ROUND 9-INCH (23-CM) CAKE

Preheat the oven to 325°F (160°C). Grease a round 9-inch (23-cm) cake pan and line the bottom with parchment paper.

In a medium saucepan, heat the sugar, water and vanilla and bring to a boil. Once the sugar has dissolved, add the almonds and cook the mixture for 2 to 3 minutes while stirring constantly. When you feel the almonds start to thicken, remove them from the heat and stir in the butter.

In a separate bowl, lightly beat the yolks and egg to break them up. Pour the eggs into the almond batter and mix to fully combine. Stir in the amaretto. Transfer the batter to the prepared pan and bake for 25 to 30 minutes, or until the cake has browned nicely and is firm to the touch. Let the cake cool completely before removing it from the pan and dusting generously with confectioners' sugar.

Tip: I recommend using good-quality free-range eggs in order to get the best color from the yolks. For a nonalcoholic version, swap the amaretto for 1 teaspoon of almond extract.

PECAN & BURNT HONEY CAKE

Burnt honey is essentially just caramelized honey, heated until the color turns a deep, dark brown with a slight smoky flavor, deep caramel notes and a hint of bitterness. The honey flavor becomes more intensified and, in this cake, sits perfectly against the crunchy, toasted pecans.

YIELD: 1 ROUND 6-INCH (15-CM) LAYER CAKE

FOR THE CAKE

1 cup (100 g) finely chopped pecans

½ cup (115 g) unsalted butter, divided

1½ cups (190 g) all-purpose flour

2 tsp (10 g) baking powder

1 cup (200 g) superfine/caster sugar

2 eggs

¾ cup (180 ml) milk

2 tsp (10 ml) vanilla extract

Preheat the oven to 350°F (180°C). Grease two round 6-inch (15-cm) cake pans and line the bottoms with parchment paper.

To make the cake, toast the pecans by adding them to a frying pan with 1 teaspoon of the butter over medium heat. Toast the nuts for a few minutes, stirring frequently until they become fragrant. Remove them from the heat and set aside to cool. Sift together the flour and baking powder in a medium bowl and set aside. Using a stand mixer or electric whisk, beat the remaining butter and sugar together for 3 to 5 minutes, or until pale and creamy. Add the eggs one at a time, beating well after each addition and scraping down the sides of the bowl every now and again. With the mixer still running, pour in half of the flour mix and beat until just combined. Pour in the milk and vanilla, followed by the remaining flour.

Fold in the pecans, and then divide the batter equally between the two prepared pans. Bake for 32 to 38 minutes, or until the cakes have browned nicely, and a toothpick inserted into the center comes out clean. Let the cakes cool for 10 minute before turning them out onto a wire rack. When the cakes are completely cool, wrap them in plastic wrap and place in the fridge to firm up.

Scant 1 cup (150 ml) honey, plus extra for serving

1 cup (225 g) unsalted butter

½ tsp salt

1⅓ cups (170 g) confectioners' sugar

¼ cup (60 ml) warm milk

½ cup (50 g) pecans, to decorate

To make the frosting, heat the honey in a large saucepan over medium heat. The honey will begin to caramelize, and the color will change into a very dark brown with a faint burnt sugar smell. At this point, remove it from the heat and stir in the butter and salt until completely melted. Let the honey butter cool to room temperature before moving it to the fridge to firm up. Once the honey is cool and has a consistency of softened butter, add it to the bowl of a stand mixer and beat for 3 to 5 minutes, or until the honey is smooth and light. Pour in the sugar and continue to beat for 5 minutes to get a thick buttercream. Beat in the milk to loosen the mixture.

Remove the cakes from the fridge and level the tops with a serrated knife if they are domed. Slice each cake into two, giving you four thin layers. Place one layer onto a cake board and put the board on a turntable (if using). Add a scoop of the burnt honey buttercream and use an offset spatula to spread it out evenly, pushing it all the way to the edge (it's fine if it spills over). Repeat with the next two layers. Once you get to the last layer, place this cake topside down for a completely flat top.

Frost the tops and sides of the cake, using a bench scraper to smooth as you go along. Stick the cake in the fridge to firm up for 20 minutes before adding another layer of buttercream to the tops and sides. Go for a thin layer of buttercream if you want a semi-naked look or a thicker layer if you want it all covered. Top with extra pecans and a drizzle of honey.

PEANUT BUTTER BANANA BREAD

4 small ripe bananas, divided

3 tbsp (50 g) smooth peanut butter

½ cup (120 ml) vegetable oil

5 tbsp (75 ml) almond or soy milk

1 tsp vanilla extract

2⅓ cups (300 g) all-purpose flour

¾ cup (175 g) light brown sugar

2 tsp (10 g) baking powder

½ tsp cinnamon

Pinch of salt

I believe that a good banana bread should be part of every baker's repertoire. As soon as you spot those black bananas in the fruit bowl, you should know what to do. This version happens to be vegan, which was by no means intentional. Swirling in some peanut butter adds a sweet-and-salty contrast that works so well. You could sub in almond butter for a mellower flavor, or even hazelnut butter would be welcome here. I do think this tastes better the next day (if it can last that long), as it gives the flavors time to mingle with each other. My favorite way to eat this is lightly toasted to crisp up the edges with a generous spread of salted butter.

YIELD: 6–8 SERVINGS

Preheat the oven to 350°F (180°C). Grease a 2-pound (900-g) loaf pan and line the bottom with parchment paper.

In a large bowl, use a fork to mash 3 bananas. Mix in the peanut butter, oil, milk and vanilla and set aside. In a separate bowl, whisk together the flour, sugar, baking powder, cinnamon and salt. Pour the banana mixture into the dry ingredients and stir gently until just combined.

Slice the remaining banana in half lengthwise. Pour the batter into the loaf pan and gently place the sliced banana on top without overlapping the slices or pushing them into the batter. Bake for 45 to 50 minutes, or until well risen and a toothpick inserted into the center comes out clean. Leave to cool completely before slicing.

Tip: For some added texture, use a crunchy peanut butter instead of smooth or fold in chopped, roasted peanuts before baking.

HAZELNUT & TAHINI CARAMEL CAKE

My obsession with tahini knows no bounds. It's been a well-used staple in my cupboard for years thanks to its versatility and creamy nuttiness. I incorporate it into just about anything from a classic hummus to this tahini caramel, which I always have a jar of on standby. It starts off expectedly sweet but deepens rather quickly into this almost savory, buttery delight. With the caramel folded into the cream cheese frosting as well as an extra drizzle on top for good measure, I always find this cake hard to share.

YIELD: 1 ROUND 8-INCH (20-CM) CAKE

FOR THE CAKE

½ cup (70 g) blanched hazelnuts

¾ cup (175 ml) sunflower oil, or any flavorless oil

¾ cup (175 g) light muscovado sugar

3 eggs

1 tsp vanilla extract

1⅓ cups (175 g) all-purpose flour

½ tbsp (8 g) baking powder

¼ tsp baking soda

½ tsp cinnamon

Pinch of ground cloves

FOR THE TAHINI CARAMEL

1 cup (200 g) superfine/caster sugar

¼ cup (50 g) unsalted butter, softened

⅔ cup (160 ml) heavy cream, at room temperature

½ tsp flaky sea salt

2 tbsp (40 g) tahini

FOR THE FROSTING

½ cup (100 g) unsalted butter, softened

¾ cup (100 g) confectioners' sugar

¾ cup (180 g) cream cheese

Toasted hazelnuts, chopped

Toasted sesame seeds, as desired

Preheat the oven to 350°F (180°C). Grease a round 8-inch (20-cm) cake pan and line with parchment paper.

To make the cake, place the hazelnuts on a baking tray and roast in the oven for 10 minutes. Let them cool and set aside a spoonful to use for decoration. Pulse the remaining hazelnuts in a food processor until fine. Set aside. In a large mixing bowl, whisk together the oil and sugar until combined. Mix in the eggs and vanilla, followed by the flour, baking powder, baking soda, cinnamon and cloves. Stir the mixture gently and briefly before pouring the batter into the prepared cake pan. Bake for 45 to 50 minutes, or until the cake is well risen and a toothpick inserted comes out clean. Leave the cake to cool in the pan for 10 minutes before turning it out onto a wire rack to cool completely.

To make the tahini caramel, heat the sugar gently in a medium saucepan. The edges will start to melt first. Stir every so often with a rubber spatula. The sugar will clump but will eventually melt down into a deep golden liquid. Add the butter and stir continuously until fully melted. The caramel will bubble up rapidly so be very careful. Slowly pour in the cream and stir. Let the caramel come to a boil for a minute before removing from the heat. Stir in the salt and tahini and leave to cool before using.

To make the frosting, beat the butter and sugar with an electric whisk or stand mixer until smooth. Add the cream cheese and beat until combined, followed by approximately ½ cup (100 g) of the tahini caramel.

Spread the frosting evenly on top of the cake using an offset spatula or the back of a spoon, leaving the sides unfrosted. Drizzle with some more caramel and top with extra chopped hazelnuts and toasted sesame seeds.

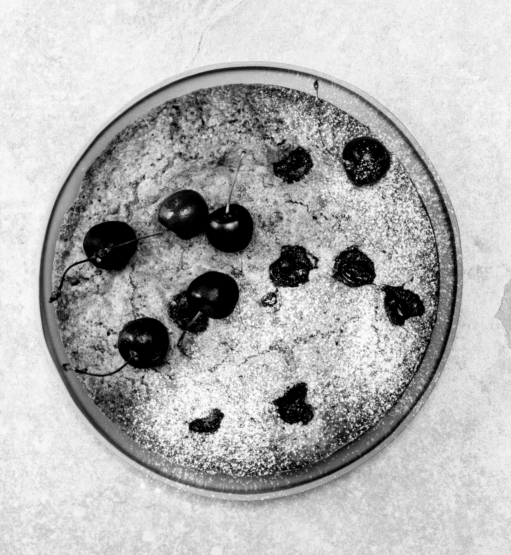

PISTACHIO–CHERRY CAKE

1½ cups (175 g) shelled pistachios

²/₃ cup (150 g) unsalted butter

³/₄ cup plus 2 tbsp (175 g) superfine/caster sugar

1 tsp vanilla bean paste

2 eggs

²/₃ cup (80 g) all-purpose flour

1 tsp baking powder

1 tbsp (15 ml) sour cream

²/₃ cup (100 g) fresh pitted cherries, plus extra to decorate

Confectioners' sugar, to dust

Pistachios are my favorite nut; I can very easily work my way through a whole bag, leaving a trail of broken shells as evidence, so naturally this is a cake that I make quite often. As a result of the high nut-to-flour ratio, you end up with a cake that has slightly crisp-chewy edges and a squidgy middle. And with the juicy cherries running all the way through, this makes for a perfect teatime treat.

YIELD: 1 ROUND 8-INCH (20-CM) CAKE

Preheat the oven to 350°F (180°C). Grease a round 8-inch (20-cm) cake pan and line with parchment paper.

Add the pistachios to a food processor and pulse until you have a fine powder. Set aside.

Using a stand mixer or electric whisk, beat the butter, sugar and vanilla for 3 to 5 minutes, or until pale and creamy. Add the eggs one at a time, beating well after each addition and scraping down the sides of the bowl every so often. Add the flour, baking powder and ground pistachios, mixing on low speed until just combined. Stir in the sour cream before transferring the batter to the prepared pan. Smooth the surface of the batter with an offset spatula and arrange the cherries randomly on top without pressing them into the batter.

Bake for 32 to 38 minutes, or until the cake is well browned and a toothpick inserted into the center comes out clean. Let the cake cool for 10 minutes before removing from the pan and setting on a wire rack. Once the cake is completely cool, use a sieve to dust lightly with confectioners' sugar and top with extra cherries.

HAZELNUT, PEAR & ESPRESSO CAKE

2/3 cup (80 g) blanched hazelnuts, plus extra to decorate

3 eggs

3/4 cup plus 2 tbsp (175 g) superfine/caster sugar

1 tsp vanilla extract

1 1/3 cups (175 g) all-purpose flour

1 1/2 tsp (8 g) baking powder

2 tsp (10 g) instant espresso powder

3/4 cup (175 g) unsalted butter, melted

4 Bosc or Conference pears, divided

Fruit and nuts have made happy partners for centuries, and this cake is no exception. The layered, thinly sliced pears sitting on top are so inviting and bring a gentle sweetness to the nutty coffee cake. Hazelnuts, unlike most other nuts, can actually dry out a cake very quickly, so I've simply folded them into the batter instead of grinding them down.

YIELD: 1 ROUND 9-INCH (23-CM) CAKE

Preheat the oven to 375°F (190°C). Grease the bottom and sides of a round 9-inch (23-cm) cake pan and line the bottom with parchment paper.

Toast the hazelnuts on a baking tray in the oven for 10 minutes, and then leave them to cool. Turn the oven down to 350°F (180°C).

In a mixing bowl, whisk together the eggs, sugar and vanilla until combined. Stir in the flour, baking powder and espresso powder and mix well before pouring in the butter and combining until smooth.

Peel, core and finely dice 2 pears and roughly chop three-quarters of the hazelnuts. Gently fold them into the batter and pour into the prepared pan. Cut the remaining 2 pears in half, with the skin left on, and use a teaspoon or melon baller to spoon out the cores. Slice them thinly and then place them on top of the cake, overlapping a few at a time. Sprinkle on the remaining hazelnuts. Bake for 40 to 45 minutes, or until the cake is well risen and firm to the touch. Leave to cool in the pan for 10 minutes before turning it out onto a wire rack to cool completely.

ALMOND BRITTLE CAKE

FOR THE CAKE

1¼ cups (150 g) all-purpose flour

1 tsp baking powder

¼ tsp ground cardamom

3 eggs

¾ cup (150 g) superfine/caster sugar

⅓ cup (75 ml) buttermilk

⅓ cup (70 g) unsalted butter, melted

FOR THE TOPPING

1⅓ cups (150 g) flaked almonds

½ cup (120 g) salted butter (or if using unsalted add a ¼ tsp of flaked sea salt)

½ cup plus 1 tbsp (120 g) light brown sugar

3 tbsp (45 ml) heavy cream

½ tsp vanilla extract

The audible crack that comes from slicing into the outer brittle layer of this cake is most satisfying. There's a wonderful game of contrasts happening here with the soft, cushion-like sponge laying beneath an armor of flaked almonds bound together with a buttery caramel. This cake is my version of the popular Scandinavian *toscakaka*. When making the cake, it might feel a little odd to place something that feels quite heavy on top of a cake that is just set, but follow through confidently and you'll be rewarded greatly.

YIELD: 1 ROUND 9-INCH (23-CM) CAKE

Preheat the oven to 350°F (180°C). Grease a springform or loose-bottomed 9-inch (23-cm) cake pan and line the bottom with parchment paper.

To make the cake, sift together the flour, baking powder and cardamom in a small bowl and set aside. Using a stand mixer or electric whisk, whisk the eggs and sugar together for 5 minutes, or until the eggs are thick and pale. The eggs need to reach ribbon stage: when you lift up the whisk attachment, the batter should leave a trail on the surface that holds its shape for a few seconds before dissolving back into itself.

Gently fold in half of the flour with a rubber spatula, being careful not to knock out too much air. Pour in the buttermilk and continue to fold the batter until the buttermilk is fully incorporated. Fold in the rest of the flour, ensuring there aren't any pockets of flour hiding at the bottom of the bowl. Carefully pour the melted butter down the side of the bowl and fold until incorporated. Pour the batter into the prepared pan and bake for 30 minutes, or until the cake is just set. There shouldn't be any wobble in the middle, as it needs to be firm enough to hold the weight of the almonds.

To make the topping, lightly toast the flaked almonds in a dry frying pan over medium heat for 1 to 2 minutes. Remove from the heat and allow to cool until needed. In a small saucepan, melt the butter with the sugar, cream and vanilla and bring to a boil. Cook for 2 to 3 minutes, or until it thickens slightly. Remove the saucepan from the heat and stir in the almonds, ensuring they're evenly coated.

Pour the mixture on top of the cooled cake and use an offset spatula to very gently spread it evenly over the surface. Put the cake back into the oven and bake for 15 minutes. Remove from the oven and leave to cool for a few minutes before running a palette knife around the edge of the cake to stop it from sticking to the sides of the pan. Let it cool completely before removing it from the pan and slicing.

Tip: Try mixing up the praline by using a mix of almonds and hazelnuts.

SPICES

Thanks to my mum, who cooked often, I grew up with a spice cupboard filled with jars of dried herbs, ginger, chili and plenty of obscure seeds and pods. Cooking and eating food made with complex, but delicately balanced blends of spices has been part of my life for as long as I can remember, and as a child, I would revel at the opportunity to throw a little bit of everything into the pot and hope for the best. I learned early on that flavor was king.

While we're all probably quite comfortable reaching for the black pepper or turmeric to go into our savory dishes, more often than not we rely less on these cupboard staples for our baking. But they are just as integral to our cakes and puddings as they are to our cooking. You'd be surprised how much good a pinch of mace or caraway can do for your bakes. Classic spices such as cinnamon bring a comforting familiarity to cakes such as the Spiced Sweet Potato Loaf with Cream Cheese Frosting (page 42). A handful of cardamom pods, split open and crushed, brightens up the Cardamom Tres Leches (page 46) cake in a refreshingly new way. The deep red flecks of sumac in the Sumac, Spelt & Apple Cake (page 54) bring a unique citrusy dimension that may at first feel unfamiliar but will quickly become one you return to again and again.

I do prefer to purchase spices in their most natural state. Grinding them yourself with a pestle and mortar or a spice grinder will give you a much better flavor, especially for cardamom, black pepper and nutmeg. One of my most loved recipes in this chapter is the Hawaij Coffee Cake (page 53), which blends together my favorite spices to create something quite magical. I'd say it's worth mixing up more of the Hawaij spice mix (page 53) than you need, allowing you some extra to sprinkle into your morning coffee or to use in other bakes.

The cakes in this chapter are full of life and will get you exploring and making the most out of your spice cupboard in novel ways. I hope you'll discover some new favorites that become staples you return to year after year.

CARDAMOM CAKE WITH MULLED WINE JAM

One of the best things about the Christmas season is the ability to mull pretty much everything in sight. I've worked my way through a mulled wine plum crumble, mulled chocolate truffles and mulled fruit compotes, just to name a few. This cake is no exception with the sweet cardamom acting as a canvas for the boozy mulled wine jam. Packed with plums, black grapes, orange and plenty of spice, this is my go-to alternative Christmas cake.

YIELD: 1 ROUND 8-INCH (20-CM) LAYER CAKE

Preheat the oven to 350°F (180°C). Grease two round 8-inch (20-cm) cake pans and line the bottoms with parchment paper.

To make the cake, gently heat the milk in a saucepan with the cardamom pods and vanilla, letting it simmer for 2 minutes before removing from the heat. Cover, and let it cool for 15 minutes before straining out the pods. Sift together the flour and baking powder in a large bowl and set aside.

Using a stand mixer or electric whisk, beat the butter and sugar until pale and creamy. Add the eggs one at a time, beating well after each addition. Mix in half of the flour, beating briefly until combined, followed by the milk and remaining flour. Divide the batter evenly between the pans and bake for 35 to 40 minutes, or until a toothpick inserted into the center comes out clean. Let the cakes cool for 15 minutes in the pans before turning them out onto a wire rack to cool completely.

To make the jam, add the wine, plums, grapes, cinnamon sticks, star anise and nutmeg to a large saucepan. Cook for 10 to 15 minutes to soften the plums. Add the sugar, lemon juice and orange and boil for 12 to 20 minutes, or until it coats the back of a spoon. Remove the cinnamon sticks, star anise and orange slices and pour into a shallow tray to cool quickly. I like my jam quite chunky, but you can run yours through a food processor if you'd like.

To make the topping, beat the mascarpone and sugar in a medium bowl by hand until smooth. Fold in the cream and vanilla and chill in the fridge until you are ready to use it.

Level the cakes with a serrated knife if they aren't even. Sandwich the cakes together with half of the mascarpone and a generous spoonful or two of jam. Cover the top and sides with the remaining mascarpone. Use a bench scraper or palette knife to smooth the sides of the cake, scraping off just enough mascarpone to let the cake peek through. Add extra grapes and a few dollops of jam.

Tip: The recipe will make a little more jam than you'll need. Store what's left in a clean glass jar or tupperware for up to a month in the fridge.

FOR THE CAKE

½ cup (120 ml) milk

10 green cardamom pods, lightly crushed

2 tsp (10 g) vanilla bean paste

2¼ cups (275 g) all-purpose flour

1 tbsp (15 g) baking powder

1 cup (225 g) unsalted butter

1 cup plus 2 tbsp (225 g) superfine/caster sugar

3 eggs

FOR THE JAM

1 cup (240 ml) red wine

2½ cups (400 g) pitted and quartered plums

2 cups (200 g) black seedless grapes, plus extra to decorate

2 cinnamon sticks

1 star anise pod

¼ tsp freshly grated nutmeg

2¼ cups (450 g) granulated sugar

2 tbsp (30 ml) lemon juice

Half an orange, thickly sliced

FOR THE TOPPING

1 cup (250 g) mascarpone

1¼ cups (150 g) confectioners' sugar

⅓ cup (80 ml) heavy cream

1 tsp vanilla extract

PINK PEPPERCORN MADELEINES

½ cup (100 g) unsalted butter

2 eggs

½ cup (100 g) superfine/caster sugar

1 tbsp (15 ml) honey

2 tsp (10 ml) vanilla

¾ cup (100 g) all-purpose flour

½ tsp baking powder

Pinch of salt

2 tsp (8 g) finely ground pink peppercorns, plus extra to decorate

⅔ cup (100 g) white chocolate

These dainty little French cakes have been injected with a warm kick and depth with the addition of crushed pink peppercorns. The color alone would be enough to make me fall in love with them, but the spicy floral notes that come from the bright seeds bring a modern feel. The crisp edges of these shell-shape cakes give way to a buttery, fluffy interior. You'd be hard-pressed not to eat a tray of these on your own in quick succession, especially as they are at their best while still warm from the oven. They do go stale very quickly, but fear not, because they make the perfect partner to dunk into a cup of tea.

YIELD: 16 – 18 MADELEINES

Melt the butter in the microwave or a small saucepan and set aside to cool. In a large bowl, whisk together the eggs and sugar for 3 to 5 minutes, or until pale and thick. Beat in the honey and vanilla, followed by the melted butter. Sift the flour, baking powder and salt on top of the egg mixture and gently fold it into the eggs to get a smooth batter. Fold in the ground peppercorns. Press a sheet of plastic wrap over the bowl and chill in the fridge for at least 1 hour or up to overnight. Chilling will give the madeleines a better rise with the signature bump, so don't skip this step.

Preheat the oven to 375°F (190°C). Grease a madeleine tray with butter, making sure to get into every nook and cranny. Dust lightly with flour and shake out the excess.

Fill the madeleine tray with about a tablespoon (15 ml) of batter in each mold. There's no need to spread the batter out evenly and don't overfill the molds. Chill the tray in the fridge for 30 minutes. Bake the madeleines for 8 to 10 minutes, keeping a close eye on them, as they can brown very quickly. Once they're golden on top, remove them from the oven, let them cool slightly for a minute and transfer to a cooling rack.

While the cakes bake, melt the white chocolate in a heatproof bowl set over a pan of simmering water. Remove from the heat and let it cool slightly. When the madeleines are baked and are still warm, dip one edge into the chocolate and then sprinkle a little of the pink peppercorns on top. Eat them straight away while the chocolate is still soft.

SPICED SWEET POTATO LOAF WITH CREAM CHEESE FROSTING

2¼ cups (260 g) all-purpose flour

1 tsp baking soda

½ tsp baking powder

2 tsp (4 g) ground cinnamon

1½ tsp (3 g) ground ginger

½ tsp freshly ground nutmeg

¼ tsp cloves

¼ tsp coarsely ground caraway

¼ tsp salt

1¾ cups (350 g) cooked and peeled sweet potato

2 eggs

½ cup (120 ml) vegetable or sunflower oil

¾ cup plus 2 tbsp (180 g) superfine/caster sugar

½ cup (100 g) light brown sugar

¼ cup (60 ml) milk

1 tsp vanilla extract

FOR THE FROSTING

⅔ cup (150 g) unsalted butter, softened

1¼ cups (150 g) confectioners' sugar

¾ cup (180 g) cream cheese

Squeeze of lemon juice

Sweet potato adds an instant moistness to this loaf and is able to carry plenty of spice. The usual suspects of cinnamon and ginger make an appearance, but I have also used a little caraway, which you may not be too familiar with. Often used in rye breads, the seeds are highly aromatic with a subtle licorice and anise flavor. There's just a ¼ teaspoon of caraway in this loaf, which is enough to brighten it up and to complement the other spices. Try adding up to 1 teaspoon for more potency.

YIELD: 8–10 SERVINGS

Preheat the oven to 350°F (180°C). Grease a 2-pound (900-g) loaf pan and line with parchment paper.

To make the loaf, mix together the flour, baking soda, baking powder, cinnamon, ginger, nutmeg, cloves, caraway and salt in a large bowl. Set aside.

Beat the sweet potatoes and eggs in a bowl by hand until combined. Add the oil, superfine sugar and brown sugar and beat until smooth. Stir in the milk and vanilla and then fold in the dry ingredients. Briefly beat the batter, making sure there are no pockets of flour hiding at the bottom. Pour the batter into the prepared pan and bake for 50 to 60 minutes, or until well risen and a toothpick inserted into the center comes out clean. Let the loaf cool for 15 minutes before inverting it onto a wire rack to cool completely.

To make the frosting, beat the butter and sugar together using a stand mixer or electric whisk for 2 to 3 minutes, or until it's smooth and pale. Add the cream cheese and a squeeze of lemon juice and beat for 1 minute, or until you have a thick, creamy frosting.

Once the loaf is completely cool, generously pile the cream cheese on top and use an offset spatula to spread it evenly and thickly across the top of the cake.

PLUM & BLACK PEPPER CAKE

1 cup (225 g) unsalted butter, room temperature

1 cup plus 2 tbsp (225 g) superfine/caster sugar

½ tsp vanilla bean paste

4 tsp (8 g) coarsely ground black pepper, divided

3 eggs

½ cup (65 g) all-purpose flour, plus extra if needed

2 cups (200 g) ground almonds

1 tsp baking powder

¼ cup (60 ml) milk

4–6 ripe plums, pitted and quartered

Handful of flaked almonds

1 tbsp (15 g) apricot jam, to decorate (optional)

Crème fraîche, for serving

Black pepper partners up beautifully with a variety of fruit—in particular, plums—adding an unexpected, but welcome twist. It won't make the cake spicy but instead brings a subtle warmth that balances out the tartness of the fruit. Not wanting to hide those gorgeous plums peeking through the sponge with unnecessary frosting, I've left this cake perfectly naked, which I feel also adds to its charm. Simply serve slightly warm with a good dollop of crème fraîche.

YIELD: 8–10 SERVINGS

Preheat the oven to 350°F (180°C). Grease a springform or loose-bottomed 9-inch (23-cm) cake pan and line the bottom with parchment paper.

Using a stand mixer or electric whisk, beat the butter, sugar, vanilla and 2 teaspoons (4 g) of the black pepper until pale and fluffy. Beat in the eggs one at a time, and if the mixture starts to curdle, add 1 tablespoon (8 g) of flour. In a medium bowl, sift together the flour, ground almonds, baking powder and 1 teaspoon of black pepper. Add this gradually into the butter mixture, followed by the milk, and gently stir until combined before pouring the batter into the prepared pan. Arrange the plum quarters on top, working your way around without pushing them too much into the batter. Sprinkle on the remaining black pepper and the flaked almonds.

Bake for 45 to 50 minutes, or until a toothpick inserted into the center of the cake comes out clean. Cool for 15 minutes in the pan before turning it out onto a wire rack to cool. Brush with some warmed apricot jam, if using, to give the cake a glazed finish before serving warm or cold, with a dollop of crème fraîche.

CARDAMOM TRES LECHES

½ cup (115 g) unsalted butter

1 cup (240 ml) milk

1½ tsp (3 g) freshly ground cardamom

1 (14-oz [397-g]) can condensed milk

1⅓ cups (330 ml) evaporated milk

¾ cup (180 ml) heavy cream

2 cups (250 g) all-purpose flour

2 tsp (10 g) baking powder

¼ tsp salt

4 eggs

1½ cups (300 g) superfine/caster sugar

2 tsp (10 ml) vanilla extract

FOR THE TOPPING

1¼ cups (300 ml) heavy cream

2 tbsp (20 g) confectioners' sugar

1 tsp vanilla extract

1 tsp cocoa powder, to dust

This isn't a cake that's widely known in the U.K., but is quite popular in the United States and originates from Latin America. Soaked in a mix of heavy cream, condensed milk and evaporated milk, it's a simple cake that's rich in flavor. Cardamom is one of my favorite spices, and the fresh, citrusy fragrance works beautifully here to cut through some of the creaminess to brighten things up. Make this ahead of time for ease and top with the whipped cream right before serving.

YIELD: 16 SERVINGS

Preheat the oven to 325°F (170°C). Butter and flour the base of a 9 x 13–inch (23 x 33–cm) baking dish.

Add the butter, milk and cardamom to a medium saucepan and heat until the butter is melted. Set aside to cool completely.

In a large jug, pour in the condensed milk, evaporated milk and cream and stir to combine. Set aside.

Sift together the flour, baking powder and salt. Using a stand mixer fitted with the whisk attachment or an electric whisk, beat the eggs, sugar and vanilla on high speed for 5 to 7 minutes, or until the eggs have tripled in volume. With the mixer still running on low, slowly pour in the cooled cardamom butter and milk. Add the flour in two batches to get a smooth batter. Pour the batter into the baking dish and bake for 35 to 40 minutes, or until the sponge springs back when touched and a toothpick inserted comes out clean.

Let the cake cool for 5 minutes before poking plenty of holes across the top of the cake with a toothpick. Pour the condensed milk mixture carefully on top of the cake, pausing every so often to let the milk sink into the holes. It may seem like far too much liquid, but the cake will absorb it all! Let the cake sit for 20 minutes before transferring to the fridge to chill for at least 4 hours, but ideally overnight. When you're ready to serve, let the cake come to room temperature for 30 minutes to 1 hour first.

To make the topping, whip together the cream, sugar and vanilla in a large bowl until you reach a spreadable consistency. Spread the cream evenly on top of the cake with a palette knife and dust with the cocoa powder.

MASALA–CHAI CARROT CAKE

FOR THE CAKE

2 English breakfast tea bags

¼ cup (60 ml) boiling water

2¾ cups (350 g) all-purpose flour

1½ tsp (8 g) baking powder

½ tsp baking soda

¼ tsp salt

1½ tsp (4 g) ground cinnamon

1 tsp ground ginger

¼ tsp ground cloves

¼ tsp freshly ground black pepper

½ tsp ground cardamom

1¾ cups (375 g) light muscovado sugar

4 eggs

1½ cups (350 ml) vegetable or sunflower oil

3–3¼ cups (350 g) grated carrots

FOR THE FROSTING

⅔ cup (150 g) unsalted butter, softened

1 cup (130 g) confectioners' sugar

1½ cups (340 g) cream cheese

8–12 walnut halves, to decorate

Carrot cake was one of the first cakes I learned how to make. It's an impressive, but really easy, one-bowl cake that doesn't require a lot of technique, and so it's always a bake that I recommend for beginners.

Since first baking this years ago, it has gone through numerous iterations and reworkings to become what it is today: a moist crumb full of warm spices and a not-too-sweet cream cheese. The masala-chai spices add so much more depth than a traditional carrot cake, which usually just relies on a bit of cinnamon to lift it up. While other more flashy and fanciful cakes come along every now and then to steal my attention, this carrot cake is the trusty friend I return to again and again.

YIELD: 1 ROUND 8-INCH (20-CM) LAYER CAKE

Preheat the oven to 350°F (180°C). Grease two round 8-inch (20-cm) cake pans and line the bottoms with parchment paper.

To make the cake, add the tea bags to a mug of the boiling water and let them steep for 5 minutes before discarding the bags. In a large bowl, whisk together the flour, baking powder, baking soda, salt, cinnamon, ginger, cloves, pepper and cardamom. Set aside. In a separate bowl, add the sugar, eggs and tea, mixing until combined before stirring in the oil. Tip in the carrots and fold them in so they're evenly distributed. Fold in the flour mixture until just incorporated, making sure there are no pockets of flour hiding near the bottom.

Divide the batter evenly between the two pans and bake for 35 to 40 minutes, or until the cakes are nicely browned and a toothpick inserted into the center comes out clean. Let the cakes cool completely in the pans before turning them out onto a wire rack.

To make the frosting, using an electric whisk, beat the butter and sugar for 3 to 5 minutes, or until pale and smooth. Add the cream cheese and beat until just combined.

To assemble, place one cake layer on a cake board or cake stand. Spoon one-third of the cream cheese on top and push the frosting right to the edges. Place the second cake topside down in order to give you a flat top. Add the rest of the frosting, spreading it out evenly with a palette knife or offset spatula. Scatter the walnuts on top of the cake.

NUTMEG CUSTARD CAKE DOUGHNUTS

FOR THE DOUGHNUTS

2 cups (250 g) all-purpose flour

½ cup plus 2 tbsp (120 g) superfine/caster sugar

2 tbsp (20 g) custard powder

1½ tsp (8 g) baking powder

¼ tsp baking soda

Pinch of salt

½ tsp ground nutmeg

2 eggs

Scant 1 cup (230 ml) milk

1 tsp vanilla extract

¼ cup (60 g) unsalted butter, melted

1 tbsp (15 ml) vegetable or sunflower oil

FOR THE GLAZE

1½ cups (200 g) confectioners' sugar

2 tsp (10 g) custard powder

1 tbsp (15 g) unsalted butter, melted

1 tsp vanilla extract

¼ cup (60 ml) milk, divided

Freshly ground nutmeg

These doughnuts were inspired by the flavors of a nostalgic British favorite: an egg custard tart. Thick, silky custard sitting in a pastry shell with a generous dusting of nutmeg brings back memories of lazy Sunday afternoons spent scoffing down one of them on the sofa while watching back-to-back episodes of *Come Dine with Me*. Turning those tarts into doughnuts was so much fun. I added some custard powder to the nutmeg-scented baked doughnuts, which, along with the custard glaze, makes them taste just as good as those tarts, if not better. These are infinitely easier to make than typical fried doughnuts and come together in a fraction of the time, perfect for when that doughnut craving hits.

YIELD: 12 DOUGHNUTS

Preheat the oven to 350°F (180°C). Grease a doughnut pan well with butter.

To make the doughnuts, mix together the flour, sugar, custard powder, baking powder, baking soda, salt and nutmeg in a large bowl. In a medium bowl, whisk together the eggs, milk and vanilla. Stir in the melted butter and oil and pour this into the dry ingredients. Stir gently until just incorporated, being careful not to overmix. Transfer the batter to a large, disposable piping bag (or food bag) and snip off the end. Pipe the batter into the doughnut pan, filling each hole about two-thirds of the way up. Bake in the oven for 10 to 12 minutes, or until the doughnuts spring back to the touch. Let them cool for a few minutes before moving them to a wire rack to cool completely. Repeat until you have used all of your batter.

To make the glaze, mix together the sugar and custard powder in a wide-but-shallow dish. Add the melted butter, vanilla and half of the milk, whisking to remove any lumps. Add more milk a little at a time until you have a consistency that's thick enough to coat the back of a spoon. If the glaze gets too thin, you can add a little more sugar. Dip one side of each doughnut into the glaze and dust with the nutmeg.

HAWAIJ COFFEE CAKE

FOR THE HAWAIJ
SPICE MIX

2½ tbsp (15 g) cardamom, roughly ground from the seeds of 12–15 pods

3 tbsp (15 g) ground ginger

½ tsp ground cinnamon

¼ tsp cloves

¼ tsp nutmeg

FOR THE COFFEE CAKE

¾ cup (175 g) unsalted butter, room temperature

¾ cup, plus 2 tbsp (175 g) superfine/caster sugar

3 eggs

1⅓ cups (175 g) all-purpose flour, plus extra if needed

1 tbsp (15 g) Hawaij

2 tsp (10 g) baking powder

Pinch of salt

1½ tbsp (18 g) espresso powder dissolved in 1 tbsp (15 ml) of hot water

FOR THE TOPPING

1 cup (250 g) mascarpone

2 tsp (10 g) espresso powder

2 tbsp (15 g) confectioners' sugar

2 tbsp (30 ml) coffee-flavored liqueur, optional

½ cup (120 ml) heavy cream

Combining spices to create something new is a skill I've grown up with, watching my mum and aunties effortlessly balance layers of spices. Hawaij is a beautifully fragrant Yemeni blend of some of my most loved spices. While savory Hawaij is commonly used in stews and soups, the sweeter aromatic version is traditionally sprinkled into coffee. Ratios vary from recipe to recipe for the delicate mix of cardamom, ginger, nutmeg, cinnamon and cloves, so do feel free to use this as a guide and play around to create your own unique blend. The Hawaij recipe below will make more than you need for this recipe, but I always enjoy having extra on hand to sprinkle into my morning coffee.

YIELD: 1 SQUARE 8-INCH (20-CM) CAKE

Preheat the oven to 350°F (180°C). Grease a square 8-inch (20-cm) cake pan and line the bottom with parchment paper.

To make the spice mix, blend together the cardamom, ginger, cinnamon, cloves and nutmeg in a small bowl and set aside. You'll only need 1 tablespoon (15 g) for this cake.

To make the cake, beat the butter and sugar in a large bowl or the bowl of a stand mixer for 4 to 5 minutes, or until pale and creamy. Add the eggs one at a time, making sure to beat well after each addition. Add 1 tablespoon (8 g) of flour if the mixture starts to curdle. In a medium bowl, mix together the flour, Hawaij, baking powder and salt. Add this to the butter mixture and beat on low speed until smooth and just combined. Stir in the espresso powder mixture and pour the batter into the prepared pan. Bake for 25 to 30 minutes, or until a toothpick inserted comes out clean. Leave it to cool in the pan for 5 minutes before turning it out onto a wire rack to cool completely.

To make the topping, beat the mascarpone in a small bowl until smooth. Pour in the espresso powder, sugar and liqueur, if using, and beat for 1 minute, or until combined. Pour in the cream and whisk until it just reaches a thick, spreading consistency. Be careful not to overwhip, as it may split.

Spread the topping generously on top of the cake and create swoops and swirls by using the back of a spoon. Slowly sweep your spoon or offset spatula back and forth across the cake, leaving about a ½ inch (1.3 cm) around the edges.

Tips: Chocolate-covered coffee beans or cacao nibs are a great, simple addition to decorate with if you can get your hands on them. This recipe could also be baked in two 6-inch (15-cm) cake pans for 20 to 25 minutes before being sandwiched together and topped with the mascarpone to give you a cake with a little more height.

SUMAC, SPELT & APPLE CAKE

Sumac is a Middle Eastern spice with a tart, lemony flavor and the most beautiful deep red color. More commonly used in savory dishes, its citrus fragrance also works just as well in a sweet cake. The spelt flour gives this vegan number a rustic look and nutty taste, producing a delightfully crunchy crust that hides a soft, moist crumb underneath, with chunks of sweet apple running all the way through.

YIELD: 8–10 SERVINGS

FOR THE APPLESAUCE

2 large Granny Smith or Bramley apples, peeled, cored and roughly chopped

1 tbsp (15 ml) lemon juice

½ cup (120 ml) water

FOR THE LOAF

1²/₃ cups (200 g) wholemeal spelt flour

Scant ½ cup (50 g) ground almonds

1 tbsp (15 g) sumac

1 tsp baking powder

1 tsp baking soda

¼ cup (60 ml) sunflower oil

½ cup plus 2 tbsp (120 g) superfine/caster sugar

1½ cups (200 g) applesauce

3 Braeburn apples, peeled, cored and diced into small chunks

FOR THE DRIZZLE

½ cup (60 g) confectioners' sugar

1 tbsp (15 ml) lemon juice

Sumac, to dust

Preheat the oven to 350°F (180°C). Grease a 1-pound (450-g) loaf pan and line with parchment paper.

To make the applesauce, add the apple pieces to a saucepan with the lemon juice and water. Let them simmer for 10 to 12 minutes, or until they have completely softened. Remove from the heat and mash the apples with a fork until smooth. You will need roughly 1½ cups (200 g) for this recipe.

To make the cake, mix together the flour, almonds, sumac, baking powder and baking soda in a large bowl and set aside. In a medium bowl, combine the oil, sugar and applesauce.

Add the wet ingredients into the dry ingredients and stir gently, ensuring there are no lumps of flour. The batter will be fairly thick. Mix in the chopped apples and pour the batter into the prepared loaf pan. Bake for 45 to 50 minutes, or until a toothpick inserted comes out clean. Leave to cool completely in the pan before turning it out.

To make the drizzle, mix the sugar and lemon juice in a medium bowl until it's thick enough to coat the back of a spoon. If it's too thin, add some more sugar or loosen it up by adding more lemon juice. Once the cake is completely cool, use a teaspoon to drizzle the icing and sprinkle on a little more sumac.

CINNAMON LOAF WITH ESPRESSO BUTTER

FOR THE LOAF

$^2/_3$ cup (160 ml) milk

2 tsp (10 ml) vanilla extract

4 cinnamon sticks

$2^1/_3$ cups (300 g) all-purpose flour

$1^1/_2$ tsp (8 g) baking powder

$1^1/_2$ tsp (4 g) ground cinnamon

$^1/_4$ tsp salt

1 cup (225 g) unsalted butter

$1^1/_4$ cups (250 g) superfine/caster sugar

4 eggs

FOR THE ESPRESSO BUTTER

2 tsp (10 g) espresso powder, dissolved in 2 tbsp (30 ml) hot water, cooled to room temperature

$^2/_3$ cup (150 g) salted butter, softened

1 tbsp (15 ml) honey

Cinnamon is one spice that we're all familiar with. From our first cinnamon swirl to a cinnamon-scented apple pie, it's that comforting, warm and reliable friend that greets you with the best hug every time you meet. While it usually plays a backseat in most cakes, often muddled with lots of other spices, this loaf gives it the opportunity to really shine with a cinnamon-infused milk and ground cinnamon in the batter. This loaf is perfect toasted with a smidge of whipped espresso butter to balance some of the sweetness.

YIELD: 8–10 SERVINGS

Preheat the oven to 325°F (160°C). Grease a narrow 5 x 12$^1/_2$-inch (13 x 32-cm) loaf pan and line with parchment paper, leaving an overhang of about $^3/_4$ inch (2 cm) on each side.

To make the loaf, add the milk, vanilla and cinnamon sticks to a small saucepan and simmer gently until the milk is hot to the touch. Remove from the heat, cover and let it steep and cool for 15 minutes. Sift together the flour, baking powder, ground cinnamon and salt in a bowl and set aside. Using a stand mixer or electric whisk, beat the butter and sugar for 3 to 5 minutes, or until pale and creamy. Add the eggs one at a time, beating well after each addition. Turn the mixer speed down to low and add the flour and milk mixture, in alternate batches, starting and ending with the flour. Pour the batter into the prepared pan and bake for 45 to 50 minutes, or until the cake is well risen and a toothpick inserted into the center comes out clean. Let the cake cool completely in the pan before turning it out onto a wire rack.

To make the espresso butter, mix the espresso powder–infused water with the butter and honey. Whip with an electric whisk for 2 to 3 minutes, or until it's pale and fluffy. Serve on top of each slice of the cinnamon loaf.

GOLDEN TURMERIC CAKE

1 tbsp (20 g) tahini

1 tbsp (10 g) black sesame seeds

1 tbsp (10 g) white sesame seeds

¾ cup (95 g) all-purpose flour

¾ cup (95 g) semolina flour

1 tsp turmeric

¾ tsp baking powder

¾ cup (150 g) superfine/caster sugar

Scant ⅔ cup (150 ml) milk

¼ cup (60 ml) vegetable or sunflower oil

1 tsp orange blossom water

Yellow like the sun, the sight of this cake always brings a smile to my face. Inspired by the Lebanese Sfouf cake, this isn't one you turn to when you need a sugar fix. I might even go so far as to say it's almost savory in flavor from the turmeric and mix of sesame seeds, which is why I love it as part of a weekend brunch spread.

YIELD: 6–8 SERVINGS

Preheat the oven to 350°F (180°C). Use the tahini to "grease" the inside of a 7-inch (18-cm) savarin or tube pan. Mix the black and white sesame seeds together and sprinkle them evenly into the pan.

In a large bowl, add the flour, semolina, turmeric, baking powder and sugar. Whisk to combine. Make a well in the center and pour in the milk, oil and orange blossom water. Mix until you have a smooth batter, and then pour into the prepared cake pan. Bake for 30 to 40 minutes, or until a toothpick inserted comes out clean. Leave the cake to cool for 10 minutes in the pan before inverting it onto a wire rack to cool. Serve while still a little warm with a strong cup of coffee.

Tip: If you're not using a savarin or tube pan, the cake can be baked in a 7-inch (18-cm) square pan. Grease the base with tahini, which will both prevent sticking and add extra flavor, but add the sesame seeds on top of the batter instead of underneath.

CHOCOLATE

Good and faithful chocolate—a constant friend in times of joy, sadness and even heartbreak. I have been known to demolish a box of chocolates all on my own, and I'm not ashamed to admit it! To say that I love chocolate is an understatement. It might possibly be one of the most exciting ingredients in a baker's pantry, and whether it's in the form of a silky ganache, swirled into buttercream or just a plain square of Cadbury, you'd be hard-pressed to go wrong with chocolate.

A couple of years ago, I was lucky enough to visit Ghana with a charity called Compassion International. On our last day, I stumbled across something large, green and orange-tinged about the size of a rugby ball. I came to learn that it was a cacao pod and was fascinated that this was the very first stage of what could soon be chocolate. Going from cacao (also called cocoa beans) to the chocolate on our supermarket shelves is a painstaking and laborious process, and since then, I've been more conscious of the chocolate that I use, making every effort to buy fair trade. My chocolate of choice to bake with is Guittard, but you should use the best quality you can afford. For recipes that contain dark chocolate, I find that those with 70-percent cocoa solids work best for flavor, giving a perfect balance of sweetness and bitterness.

The recipes in this chapter are indulgent, made to lift your spirits and comfort you with a warm chocolately hug. The Hot Chocolate & Halva Pudding (page 76) is so wonderfully rich, you'll eat it straight out of the dish. A little more delicate, but by no means shy, there's the White Chocolate, Rose & Pistachio Tiramisu (page 83), which the very thought of makes me a little giddy with excitement. My chocolate recipes are layered with bold-yet-nuanced flavors, and I hope most of them will be cakes that you haven't tried before but will be delighted by. Incorporating fresh herbs, different flours and more unfamiliar ingredients brings about a modern feel, so dive head first into these recipes and be reminded of how utterly fabulous it is to have a friend like chocolate.

CHOCOLATE & SALTED PRALINE LOG

FOR THE SALTED PRALINE PASTE

1 cup (150 g) hazelnuts, blanched

½ cup (100 g) superfine/caster sugar

1½ tsp (7 g) flaky sea salt

FOR THE SPONGE

¾ cup (90 g) all-purpose flour

3 tbsp (15 g) cocoa powder

½ tsp baking powder

4 eggs

½ cup plus 2 tbsp (120 g) superfine/caster sugar

1 tsp vanilla extract

Whether you call this a yule log, Swiss roll or bûche de Noël, this is the cake for the festive season. It's decadent in every way, from the salted hazelnut praline that gets folded into a billowy cream to the feather-light chocolate sponge that gets soaked in hazelnut liqueur—all before being coated in a dark chocolate ganache and covered with thin chocolate shards. Don't be intimidated by the number of steps. I promise it'll be well worth the effort for this festive showstopper.

YIELD: 6–8 SERVINGS

Preheat the oven to 350°F (180°C).

To make the salted praline paste, place the hazelnuts on a lined baking tray and toast in the oven for 5 to 7 minutes. Keep an eye on them so they don't burn. Remove from the oven and set aside. Heat the sugar in a large saucepan over medium heat. The edges will start to melt first. Stir with a rubber spatula so the sugar melts evenly. The sugar may clump, but keep stirring and it will eventually melt. Once the caramel is completely melted and is a deep amber color, remove from the heat. Carefully pour it over the hazelnuts, trying to cover as many of them as possible. The sugar will be extremely hot at this point, so don't let it touch your skin.

Leave the praline to set until it has hardened and is cool to the touch. Break the praline into rough pieces and place in a food processor along with the salt. Pulse for 10 to 20 seconds, or until it resembles fine crumbs. Take out approximately 1 to 2 tablespoons (20 to 40 g) of the mixture and place it in a separate bowl. We'll use this when rolling up the log. Continue to process the rest of the praline for 1 to 2 minutes; you'll notice it will start to turn into a paste. Process until you have a mixture that resembles peanut butter. If your praline is stubborn and won't form a paste, add 1 tablespoon (15 ml) of a flavorless oil, such as sunflower, and continue to process to help it along. Transfer the praline paste to a bowl and set aside.

To make the sponge, grease a 9 x 13-inch (23 x 33-cm) Swiss roll pan and line it with parchment paper. Sift together the flour, cocoa powder and baking powder into a small bowl and set aside. Using a stand mixer or electric whisk, whisk together the eggs, sugar and vanilla for 5 to 7 minutes, or until pale and tripled in volume. Sieve half of the flour mix on top of the eggs and very gently fold them together. Try not to knock out too much of the air you've just incorporated. Sieve the other half of the flour on top and repeat the folding process, making sure there aren't pockets of flour hiding at the bottom. Gently pour the batter into the prepared pan and spread it out to the corners. Bake for 10 to 12 minutes, or until the sides start to shrink away from the pan. Let it cool for just a few minutes.

(Continued)

CHOCOLATE & SALTED PRALINE LOG (CONTINUED)

FOR THE FILLING

³/₄ cup (200 ml) heavy cream

1 tbsp (10 g) confectioners' sugar

1 tsp vanilla extract

4 tbsp (80 g) Salted Praline Paste

FOR THE GANACHE

1¼ cups (120 g) finely chopped 70% dark chocolate

½ cup (120 ml) heavy cream

FOR THE CHOCOLATE SHARDS

1½ cups (150 g) 70% dark chocolate

FOR ASSEMBLY

3 tbsp (45 ml) hazelnut liqueur

1–2 tbsp (20–40 g) crumbled praline (reserved from making the Salted Praline Paste)

Confectioners' sugar, for serving

Place a piece of parchment paper that's bigger than the size of the cake pan on the counter. Dust the paper generously with confectioners' sugar and invert the cake onto it. Peel away the parchment paper that the cake was baked on, trim the edges with a sharp knife and score a line about a ½ inch (1.3 cm) in, along one of the shorter edges. Don't score all the way through the sponge. Roll up the cake tightly from the edge that you scored with the parchment paper so that the paper is rolled up inside and becomes the outer layer of the cake. Leave the cake to cool completely.

To make the filling, whip together the heavy cream, sugar and vanilla until you have stiff peaks. Fold in the Salted Praline Paste and set aside.

To make the ganache, add the finely chopped chocolate to a heatproof bowl. Heat the cream in a small saucepan and bring to a simmer. Pour this over the chocolate and let it sit for 1 minute. Stir the ganache until it comes together and becomes smooth and glossy. Set it aside to thicken to a spreadable consistency.

To make the chocolate shards, place about three-quarters of the chocolate in a heatproof bowl set over a pan of simmering water, making sure the bottom of the bowl isn't touching the water. Let the chocolate melt completely before removing from the heat. Add the remaining chocolate and stir for a few minutes until it's all melted. Pour the chocolate onto a baking tray lined with parchment paper. Spread the chocolate thinly and evenly into a large rectangle and place another layer of parchment paper on top. Use your hand to carefully smooth out the paper and to remove any air bubbles. Roll the parchment up into a log, and place the chocolate in the fridge to set for 30 minutes to 1 hour. Once it's completely firm, unroll the parchment paper. As you unroll it, the chocolate will break into random-size shards. Keep these in the fridge until you're ready to use them.

To assemble, carefully unroll the cake (don't worry if it cracks a little) and brush with the hazelnut liqueur. Spread the filling evenly on top and sprinkle on the crumbled praline that we reserved earlier. Reroll the cake as tightly as you can and let it firm up in the fridge for 30 minutes. Using an offset spatula or palette knife, cover the outside of the cake with the ganache, getting it as smooth as possible. Place the shards on the ganache and overlap some of the pieces to give a bark effect. If some of the pieces don't stick, warm up the ganache a little by rubbing it with a hot spoon. Keep the cake in the fridge until you are ready to serve it and then use a small sieve to dust with confectioners' sugar.

CHOCOLATE, RYE & PASSIONFRUIT CAKE

FOR THE CURD

1 egg

1 egg yolk

½ cup (100 g) superfine/caster sugar

Pulp and seeds from 6 ripe passionfruits

1 tbsp (15 ml) lemon juice

¼ cup (50 g) unsalted butter

FOR THE CAKE

1½ cups (190 g) whole wheat flour

1½ cups (190 g) rye flour

2 cups (400 g) superfine/caster sugar

¾ cup (60 g) cocoa powder

2 tsp (10 g) baking powder

1 tsp baking soda

¼ tsp salt

1 cup (240 ml) vegetable oil

2 tsp (10 ml) vanilla extract

2 cups (480 ml) hot water

2 tbsp (30 ml) white wine vinegar

There's a real game of contrasts happening in this cake. I opted to use a mix of whole wheat and rye flour for the chocolate sponge, not in order to make this in any way a "healthy" cake, but to bring a new dimension to a classic. The rye flour gives such a pleasant, nutty flavor in addition to an earthy undertone, which isn't expected in a chocolate cake. I also love the unique coarse texture that using whole wheat flour brings. It first surprises and then delights. With a zingy passionfruit curd to brighten it all up, there's a dark chocolate buttercream to bring everything together in harmony.

YIELD: 6–8 SERVINGS

Preheat the oven to 350°F (180°C). Grease three round 8-inch (20-cm) cake pans and line the bottoms with parchment paper.

To make the curd, add the egg, yolk, sugar, passionfruit and lemon juice to a medium saucepan and heat over low heat. Whisk the mixture constantly, and it will start to thicken after 4 to 6 minutes. Once it's thick enough to coat the back of a spoon, remove from the heat and stir in the butter until melted. Transfer to a clean bowl and cover with plastic wrap, ensuring it touches the surface of the curd. Let it cool to room temperature before putting it in the fridge to chill.

To make the cake, whisk together in a large bowl the whole wheat flour, rye flour, sugar, cocoa powder, baking powder, baking soda and salt. Make a well in the center and pour in the oil, vanilla, hot water and white wine vinegar. Mix the batter by hand until it's smooth. Divide the batter evenly between the three pans and bake in the oven for 25 to 30 minutes, or until a toothpick inserted into the center comes out clean. Remove from the oven and place on a wire rack to cool completely.

(Continued)

CHOCOLATE, RYE & PASSIONFRUIT CAKE (CONTINUED)

1½ cups (150 g) 70% dark chocolate

1 cup (225 g) unsalted butter, softened

2 cups (270 g) confectioners' sugar

½ cup plus 2 tbsp (50 g) cocoa powder

To make the buttercream, melt the chocolate in the microwave in increments of 20 seconds. Set aside to cool. Using a stand mixer or electric whisk, beat the butter on medium-high speed for 3 to 5 minutes, or until it's pale and creamy. Add the sugar and cocoa powder and beat for another 5 minutes, or until the buttercream is thick and fluffy. Turn the mixer speed down to low and pour in the cooled, melted chocolate and beat for 30 seconds, or until the chocolate is fully incorporated.

To assemble the cake, make sure each cake layer is level by using a serrated knife or cake leveler to slice off any domed tops. Place one layer on a cake board or cake stand and use an ice cream scoop to measure out 2 scoops of buttercream. Spread this evenly across the cake with an offset spatula, pushing the buttercream all the way just over the edge. Add roughly 2 tablespoons (15 g) of the passionfruit curd on top of the buttercream and spread it out, leaving about 1 inch (2.5 cm) clear from the edges. Repeat with the next layer.

Place the last layer topside down to give you a completely flat top. Spread a thin layer of buttercream across the top and sides of the cake. This is the crumb coat that will trap all the stray crumbs in place. Smooth the sides as much as you can using a bench scraper or a large palette knife. Put the cake in the fridge for 20 minutes to firm up.

Spread the remaining buttercream all over the cake. Using the back of a spoon or an offset spatula, make circular motions on the buttercream before lifting up your wrist with a little flick to add some texture to the top and sides.

COCONUT, WHITE CHOCOLATE & MORINGA LOAF

FOR THE LOAF

1¹⁄₃ cups (175 g) all-purpose flour, plus extra if needed

1½ tsp (8 g) baking powder

1 cup (100 g) desiccated or shredded unsweetened coconut

³⁄₄ cup (175 g) unsalted butter

³⁄₄ cup plus 2 tbsp (175 g) superfine/caster sugar

1 tsp vanilla extract

3 eggs

¹⁄₃ cup (75 ml) plain yogurt

¹⁄₃ cup (50 g) white chocolate chips

FOR THE GANACHE

1¹⁄₄ cups (120 g) finely chopped white chocolate

1½ tsp (5 g) moringa powder

¹⁄₃ cup (80 ml) heavy cream, divided

Handful of coconut flakes, lightly toasted

Coconut cakes remind me of school lunches back in the day. Standing in the lunch line and catching wind that dessert was coconut sponge and custard was an instant way to forget why you weren't talking to your best friend. I'd be presented with the fattest wedge of fluffy sponge flecked with coconut and swimming in custard that would end up stone cold by the time I got to it. Not that it mattered. I'd still take my time, savoring every bite. For this loaf, I've taken my favorite coconut sponge, studded it with white chocolate chips and glazed it with a white chocolate moringa ganache for a creamy addition. Moringa is similar in taste and color to matcha but slightly less bitter. While I wouldn't necessarily sink a slice of this in custard, I'm sure those lunch ladies would still be proud.

YIELD: 8–10 SERVINGS

Preheat the oven to 325°F (170°C). Grease a 2-pound (900-g) loaf pan and line the bottom with parchment paper.

To make the loaf, add the flour, baking powder and coconut to a bowl and stir to combine. Using a stand mixer or electric whisk, beat the butter, sugar and vanilla for 5 minutes, or until pale and fluffy. Scrape down the sides of the bowl every so often. Add the eggs one at a time, beating well after each addition. If the mixture looks like it's starting to curdle, add 1 tablespoon (8 g) of flour. With the mixer on low, add the flour mixture, followed by the yogurt. Once incorporated, stir in the chocolate chips. Pour the batter into the prepared pan and bake for 45 to 55 minutes, or until the cake is golden brown and a toothpick inserted in the center comes out clean. Let the loaf cool for 5 minutes in the pan before inverting it upside down onto a wire rack to cool.

To make the ganache, place the chopped white chocolate in a heatproof bowl and set aside. Add the moringa powder and 1 tablespoon (15 ml) of the cream to a saucepan and whisk until there are no lumps. Pour in the rest of the cream and heat gently, bringing it to a simmer. Pour the cream over the white chocolate and let it sit for about 10 seconds before stirring to combine. If there are chunks of chocolate that haven't melted, place the bowl over a small pan of simmering water until fully melted. Let the ganache cool slightly so it can thicken up before you pour it on top of the coconut cake. Top with toasted coconut flakes.

Tips: For a slightly different look, allow the ganache to sit longer and thicken to a spreadable consistency before adding it on top of the cake. You can find moringa powder online or in some health-food stores. If you're unable to source it, matcha powder works as an alternative.

CHOCOLATE GUINNESS BUNDT WITH YOGURT GLAZE

1 cup (225 g) unsalted butter

1 cup (240 ml) Guinness Stout

½ cup plus 3 tbsp (55 g) cocoa powder

2 cups (250 g) all-purpose flour

1¾ cups (350 g) superfine/caster sugar

1½ tsp (8 g) baking soda

½ tsp salt

2 eggs

¾ cup (200 ml) plain yogurt

¾ cup (200 ml) plain yogurt

3 tbsp (20 g) confectioners' sugar

Guinness is a much-loved drink in Nigeria, with more of it consumed there than Ireland! As dark as the night, this cake would most certainly make a statement as a table centerpiece. It's a real chocolate cake for grown-ups, with a heady richness. The stout works in partnership with the chocolate to bring an earthy, velvety flavor, which is offset by the tangy yogurt. I love the contrast of the nearly black cake sitting underneath the white glaze that seeps into the grooves and valleys of the intricately shaped pan . . . a nod to that iconic frothy top on a pint of Guinness.

YIELD: 10–12 SERVINGS

Preheat the oven to 350°F (180°C). Grease a 10-cup (2.6-L) Bundt pan well with a little melted butter and dust lightly with flour, tipping out the excess. Make sure you get into every nook and cranny to ensure the cake comes out of the pan in one piece!

For the cake, simmer the butter and Guinness in a large saucepan until the butter melts. Remove from the heat and whisk in the cocoa powder until smooth. In a large bowl, whisk together the flour, sugar, baking soda and salt and set aside. Mix together the eggs and yogurt in a bowl to combine before stirring in the Guinness mixture. Pour the liquids into the dry ingredients and whisk briefly by hand to ensure there are no lumps. Pour the batter into the prepared pan and bake for 35 to 40 minutes, or until a toothpick inserted in the center comes out clean. Let the cake cool in the pan for exactly 10 minutes before inverting it onto a wire rack. If you try to remove the cake from the pan too soon or after too much time, the cake may stick to the pan.

To make the glaze, mix together the yogurt and sugar in a small bowl, ensuring there are no lumps. You should have a thin, pourable consistency. Pour this evenly over the cooled cake before serving.

Tip: To get an even glaze, pour on half of the glaze with a steady flow, then let it sit for 20 seconds before pouring on the rest.

BITTER CHOCOLATE & ROSEMARY TORTES

¼ cup (60 ml) heavy cream

2 tsp (2 g) finely chopped fresh rosemary, divided

2¼ cups (225 g) roughly chopped 70% dark chocolate

¼ cup (55 g) unsalted butter

3 eggs, separated

¼ cup (50 g) superfine/caster sugar

½ tsp flaky sea salt

Confectioners' sugar, to dust

Small but mighty is probably the best way to describe these. The perfect accompaniment to an after-dinner coffee or digestif, these little tortes are incredibly rich in chocolate and gently scented with fresh rosemary. They don't contain any flour, making them gluten-free, and I love making these in pretty little tart cases so they're easier to serve, as there's no need to slice.

YIELD: 12 TORTES

Preheat the oven to 350°F (180°C). Grease 12 miniature fluted tart cases and lightly dust with flour, tapping out the excess.

Gently warm the cream and 1 teaspoon of the rosemary in a small saucepan. Remove from the heat, cover and steep for 10 minutes. Place the chocolate and butter in a heatproof bowl and set it over a pan of simmering water, making sure the bottom of the bowl doesn't touch the water. Stir until fully melted and then remove from the heat.

In a medium bowl, whisk together the egg yolks and sugar until creamy and fold this into the melted chocolate followed by the cream, sea salt and the remaining chopped rosemary. In a small bowl, whip the egg whites until you have stiff peaks, and then gently fold this into the chocolate mix.

Spoon the batter into the tart cases and bake for 12 to 15 minutes, until the cakes are set around the edges but still slightly soft in the middle. Leave to cool completely and dust with confectioners' sugar before serving.

Tip: These can be baked in mini-cupcake trays for a different shape and dusted in cocoa powder for less contrast.

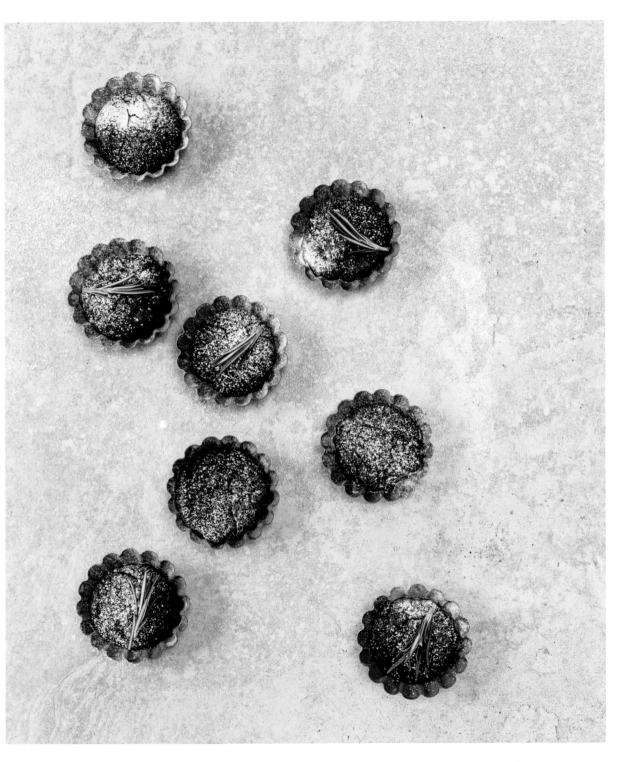

CHOCOLATE FUDGE & TAHINI CAKE

FOR THE CAKE

1/3 cup (80 g) unsalted butter

2 1/4 cups (270 g) all-purpose flour

1 1/2 cups (300 g) superfine/caster sugar

3/4 cup plus 1 tbsp (65 g) cocoa powder

1 1/2 tsp (8 g) baking powder

1 1/2 tsp (7 g) baking soda

1/2 tsp salt

2 eggs

Scant 1 cup (200 ml) milk

1 tsp vanilla extract

2/3 cup (160 ml) hot coffee (or hot water)

FOR THE BUTTERCREAM

3/4 cup plus 2 tbsp (200 g) unsalted butter, softened

2 1/2 cups (300 g) confectioners' sugar

Pinch of salt

2 tsp (10 ml) vanilla extract

4 1/2 tbsp (70 g) tahini

Scant 2 tbsp (15 g) sesame seeds, lightly toasted, to decorate

With dark, moist layers that are a little dense and rather rich, this is probably my favorite and most-baked chocolate cake recipe. It's a great base to experiment with different frostings and fillings. I've gone for tahini here, a paste made from ground sesame seeds. It has a creamy texture and a mild nuttiness that balances out the chocolate layers.

YIELD: 1 ROUND 6-INCH (15-CM) LAYER CAKE

Preheat the oven to 350°F (180°C). Grease three round 6-inch (15-cm) cake pans, and line the bottoms with parchment paper. To make the cake, melt the butter in the microwave and leave to cool. Sift together the flour, sugar, cocoa powder, baking powder, baking soda and salt in a large bowl. In a medium bowl, beat the eggs with the milk and vanilla. Pour in the melted butter and stir this into the dry ingredients. Mix well before adding the hot coffee for a smooth batter; it will be quite runny. Divide the mixture equally between your prepared cake pans and bake for 25 to 30 minutes, or until a toothpick inserted in the center comes out clean. Leave the cakes to cool for 10 minutes before turning them out onto a wire rack to cool completely.

To make the buttercream, beat the butter using a stand mixer or electric whisk for 4 to 5 minutes, or until pale and creamy. Add the sugar, salt and vanilla and beat for 3 minutes, or until you have a thick and fluffy buttercream. Pour in the tahini and beat for a few seconds to combine.

To assemble the cakes, check that each layer is level. If any are uneven, wrap them in plastic wrap and place them in the fridge to firm up for 30 minutes. This will make it easier to get a clean cut. Level the uneven layers with a sharp serrated knife or cake leveler. Place the first cake on a cake board and then put this on a turntable, if using. Add a scoop of buttercream and spread it out evenly with an offset spatula before repeating with the next layer. When you get to the last cake, place it topside down to give you a completely flat top. Add a thin layer of buttercream on the top and sides of the cake, smoothing the sides with a bench scraper or palette knife. Hold the bench scraper at a 90-degree angle, resting on the cake board and use your free hand to gently pull the turntable toward you. Don't press the bench scraper into the cake; it should just be touching the buttercream. Scrape any excess buttercream into a separate bowl. Repeat this process until your sides are smooth.

Place the cake in the fridge for 30 minutes to firm up before adding another thin layer of buttercream on the top and sides, repeating the smoothing process. To get the semi-naked look, you want some of the cake to poke through the frosting, so don't add too much buttercream. Gently press the sesame seeds onto the sides and top of the cake. I do this by pressing my fingertip firmly into the seeds so they stick to my finger and then lightly touch the cake to transfer them.

HOT CHOCOLATE & HALVA PUDDING

FOR THE CAKE

1 cup (125 g) all-purpose flour

²/₃ cup (150 g) light brown sugar

1 tsp baking powder

¼ cup (20 g) cocoa powder

½ tsp flaky sea salt

½ cup (120 ml) milk

1 egg

⅓ cup (80 g) unsalted butter, melted

1 tsp vanilla extract

½ cup (150 g) roughly chopped plain or vanilla halva

½ cup (75 g) dark chocolate chips, or roughly chopped chocolate

FOR THE SAUCE

4 tbsp (20 g) cocoa powder

²/₃ cup (150 g) light brown sugar

1 cup (250 ml) boiling water

1 tsp espresso powder

It's a rainy Wednesday, and you've had a long day. That chocolate craving hits and this is what you turn to. Hot Chocolate & Halva Pudding is my mid-week indulgence that is the best accompaniment to a Netflix catch-up while curled on the sofa. This isn't anything like what you'd call a pudding in the United States and instead has a similar texture to a steamed cake served piping hot. The cake crust is thick yet so soft it gives easily as you sink your spoon inside. Underneath lies a pool of chocolate gold produced by what can only be magic and is flecked with crumbly pieces of sesame halva—a dense Middle Eastern candy. This is best served as soon as it exits the oven, while the chocolate sauce is still swimming. And if you've had a really bad day, add a scoop of ice cream for good measure.

YIELD: SERVES   10–12

Preheat the oven to 350°F (180°C). Grease a deep 9 x 12-inch (23 x 31-cm) baking dish.

To make the cake, add the flour, sugar, baking powder, cocoa powder and salt to a large bowl and whisk to break up any lumps. In a medium bowl, combine the milk, egg, butter and vanilla and pour this into the flour mixture. Stir until the batter is smooth and without large lumps. Gently fold in the chopped halva and chocolate chips before pouring the batter into the prepared dish. Set aside.

To make the sauce, add the cocoa powder, sugar, boiling water and espresso powder to a medium bowl and stir together with a fork, removing any lumps. Pour the liquid carefully on top of the cake batter—it will look very strange at this point, but don't worry or try to mix it in. Bake for 28 to 35 minutes, or until the cake is puffy and just set. There'll be a pool of chocolate sauce underneath once you break the crust. Serve hot.

Tip: For an extra hit of sesame flavor, swirl some tahini through the batter before adding the hot water. Find halva online or in any Middle Eastern supermarket.

FLOURLESS CHOCOLATE–CHILI CAKE

$^3/_4$ cup plus 1 tbsp (190 g) unsalted butter

2 cups (190 g) 70% dark chocolate

1 tsp cayenne pepper powder

Scant $^1/_3$ cup (75 ml) espresso or strong coffee, cooled

$^1/_2$ tsp vanilla extract

3 eggs

$^2/_3$ cup (135 g) superfine/caster sugar

$^1/_2$ tsp flaky sea salt

2 tbsp (10 g) cocoa powder, to dust

This cake was inspired by the popular Swedish *kladdkaka*, which translates as "sticky cake." We deliberatly underbake this to give it the characteristically gooey interior, and as it cools, it naturally sinks and produces the most beautiful cracks. If you're someone who struggles with making a cake look "perfect," this is the one for you. The warming heat that comes from the cayenne pepper lingers just long enough to leave you wanting more.

YIELD: 1 ROUND 8-INCH (20-CM) CAKE

Preheat the oven to 350°F (180°C). Grease a springform or loose-bottomed 8-inch (20-cm) cake pan and line the bottom with parchment paper.

Melt the butter, chocolate and cayenne pepper in a small saucepan. Once the chocolate has melted, remove from the heat and stir in the coffee and vanilla. Let it cool. Using a stand mixer or electric whisk, whisk together the eggs and sugar for 3 to 5 minutes, or until thick, pale and fluffy. Pour the chocolate mixture into the eggs, add the salt and fold gently to combine. Pour the batter into the prepared pan and bake for 40 to 45 minutes, or until the cake is just baked with a slight wobble in the middle.

Remove from the oven and allow the cake to cool completely. As it cools, the surface will crack, and this is what we want! Use a small sieve to dust generously with cocoa powder before serving.

MALTED CHOCOLATE CAKE WITH BAILEYS IRISH CREAM GANACHE

1³/₄ cups (175 g) roughly chopped 70% dark chocolate

³/₄ cup (170 g) unsalted butter, room temperature

1¹/₄ cups (250 g) superfine/caster sugar

2 tsp (10 ml) vanilla extract

6 eggs, separated

3 tbsp (60 g) malt extract

1¹/₄ cups (155 g) all-purpose flour

1 tsp baking powder

1 tbsp (15 g) malted milk powder

Pinch of salt

FOR THE GANACHE

2 cups (200 g) finely chopped 70% dark chocolate

¹/₂ cup (120 ml) heavy cream

¹/₃ cup (80 ml) Baileys Irish Cream

5 tsp (25 ml) corn syrup or golden syrup

1 tbsp (15 g) unsalted butter, softened

The flavor of malt transports me back to when I was a child and would request a hot, milky cup of Horlicks or Ovaltine before bed. I'd always sneak in extra heaped teaspoons of the powder that would end up clumped in the bottom of the mug, allowing me to savor that malty goodness. With this cake, I've gone straight to the source of that nostalgic flavor by using malt extract, which looks a little like a dark, treacly honey. Now that I'm older, my nightcap of choice is likely to involve a splash of Baileys, which I have incorporated into the decadent ganache—an easy-yet-impressive topping for a cake.

YIELD: 1 ROUND 9-INCH (23-CM) CAKE

Preheat the oven to 325°F (170°C). Grease a round 9-inch (23-cm) cake pan and line the bottom with parchment paper.

To make the cake, place the chocolate in a heatproof bowl. Set the bowl over a saucepan of simmering water, making sure the base of the bowl doesn't touch the water. Melt the chocolate, stirring every so often. Set aside to cool slightly. Using a stand mixer fitted with the paddle attachment or electric whisk, beat the butter, sugar and vanilla until light and fluffy. Gradually beat in the egg yolks before stirring in the cooled, melted chocolate and malt extract. Fold in the flour, baking powder and malted milk powder to get a smooth, thick batter. In a medium bowl, whisk the egg whites and salt for 2 to 3 minutes, or until stiff. Take one-quarter of the egg whites and stir it into the chocolate batter to loosen it up. Carefully fold in the rest of the egg whites until the batter is smooth with no streaks. Scoop the batter into the cake pan and bake for 45 to 55 minutes, or until the cake is firm to the touch and a toothpick inserted in the center comes out clean. If the cake is taken out too early, it may sink in the middle.

To make the ganache, place the chopped chocolate in a bowl. Place the cream, Baileys and corn syrup in a small saucepan and heat until it's just about to come to a boil. Remove from the heat and pour the cream over the chopped chocolate, stirring until the chocolate has melted. Stir in the butter until you have a smooth and glossy ganache. Cover the ganache with plastic wrap, making sure it touches the surface of the ganache. Set it aside at room temperature to thicken to a spreadable consistency. This could take up to a couple of hours depending on the temperature of your kitchen.

Use a palette knife or offset spatula to spread a thick layer of ganache on the top and sides of the cake.

WHITE CHOCOLATE, ROSE & PISTACHIO TIRAMISU

1 cup plus 2 tbsp (140 g) all-purpose flour

1 tbsp (10 g) cornstarch

1 tsp baking powder

3 egg whites

½ cup (100 g) superfine/caster sugar, divided

2 egg yolks

¼ tsp rosewater

Confectioners' sugar, to dust

FOR THE SYRUP

Scant ½ cup (100 ml) white wine

¼ cup (50 g) superfine/caster sugar

FOR THE FILLING

3 egg yolks

¼ cup (50 g) superfine/caster sugar

3 egg whites

1½ cups (350 g) mascarpone

If there's ever a tiramisu on the menu for dessert, nine times out of ten, that's what I'll choose. Making it from scratch might seem like a lot of effort, but it's so worth it when you can customize and experiment with different flavors. This white chocolate, rose and pistachio version feels a little more elegant than the classic coffee, and despite containing plenty of mascarpone, it's deceptively light thanks to the whipped egg whites. If you're pressed for time, you can make the sponge fingers in advance—they keep for up to a week and actually work better when they're a little stale.

YIELD: 6 SERVINGS

Preheat the oven to 350°F (180°C). Line two baking trays with parchment paper.

To make the sponge fingers, sift together the flour, cornstarch and baking powder in a small bowl. Set aside. Using an electric whisk, whisk the egg whites for 1 minute, or until it gets foamy. Add half of the sugar and whisk for 2 to 3 minutes, or until you have stiff peaks. Set aside. In a medium bowl, whisk the egg yolks with the remaining sugar and rosewater for 3 to 4 minutes, or until the yolks are thick, pale and creamy. Gently fold the yolks into the whites until fully combined. Sift the flour mixture on top of the batter and carefully fold together to make a thick, smooth batter. Try not to knock out too much air.

Transfer the batter to a piping bag fitted with a plain, round nozzle and pipe sausages of 3 to 4 inches (8 to 10 cm) in length onto the baking trays. Leave about 1 inch (2.5 cm) between each sponge finger. Dust the trays of fingers very generously with confectioners' sugar and then bake for 12 to 15 minutes, or until the sponges are golden brown and firm to the touch. Let them cool completely on the trays.

To make the syrup, heat the wine and sugar in a small pan and bring to a boil. Let it simmer for 2 minutes before removing from the heat and setting aside to cool.

To make the filling, place the egg yolks and sugar in a heatproof bowl set over a pan of simmering water. Whisk constantly with an electric whisk for 4 to 6 minutes, or until the yolks are pale and thick. Remove from the heat and set aside to cool.

(Continued)

FOR ASSEMBLY

1½ cups (150 g) finely grated white chocolate

Scant ¼ cup (20 g) finely chopped pistachios

2 tbsp (10 g) dried rose petals

In a medium bowl, whisk the egg whites with an electric whisk for 3 minutes, or until stiff. (Make sure to clean the beaters!) Add the mascarpone to the egg yolks and beat briefly until smooth. Gently fold in the egg whites until fully combined. Leave this in the fridge until you are ready to assemble.

To assemble, break your sponge fingers into halves or thirds, depending on the size of your glasses. Layer the bottom of each glass with a sponge piece and drizzle some of the cooled white wine syrup on top. Add a generous spoonful of mascarpone followed by a layer of grated white chocolate and chopped pistachios. Repeat this pattern until each glass is full. Chill the tiramisu in the fridge for at least 1 hour before topping with dried rose petals and more pistachios before serving.

Tip: I've gone for individual portions here, but you can definitely make this in one large dish for a crowd. If you do, don't break the sponge fingers up but keep them whole and layer them.

STICKY GINGER CAKE WITH CARAMELIZED WHITE CHOCOLATE BUTTERCREAM

FOR THE CARAMELIZED
WHITE CHOCOLATE

2½ cups (250 g) roughly chopped white chocolate

Pinch of flaky sea salt

FOR THE CAKE

¾ cup plus 2 tbsp (200 g) unsalted butter

2 tbsp (40 g) molasses or treacle

¾ cup (180 ml) corn syrup or golden syrup

3 tbsp (45 ml) stem ginger syrup

2 tsp (10 ml) vanilla extract

1 cup (220 g) dark brown sugar

2 eggs, lightly beaten

1 cup (240 ml) milk

2¾ cups (350 g) all-purpose flour

2 tsp (10 g) baking soda

¼ cup (20 g) ground ginger

1 tsp cinnamon

Pinch of cloves

I'm a big fan of white chocolate. Although it can be a little too sweet and one dimensional for some, I'm more than happy munching on a few squares when I need a little sugar pick-me-up. Caramelizing the white chocolate, however, transforms it into something with much more depth. Think of a really creamy dulce de leche, and you're not far off. Making it requires a bit of patience, but you'll be rewarded well at the end. The creaminess and caramel flavor works well against the ginger cake—neither distracts from the other, but they each hold their own.

YIELD: 12–16 SERVINGS

Preheat the oven to 275°F (140°C).

To make the caramelized white chocolate, place the white chocolate onto a large baking tray and bake in the oven for 15 minutes, or until melted. Remove from the oven, give it a stir with an offset spatula and spread it out evenly. Return the chocolate back to the oven and continue to bake for at least 1 hour, removing and stirring every 10 minutes until it turns a dark amber color. Halfway through, the chocolate may look grainy and clumped. Don't worry about this—just keep stirring and spreading thoroughly every 10 minutes until it liquifies. Once caramelized, divide the chocolate between two bowls, with one containing about two-thirds (for the buttercream). The lesser amount is for drizzling on the completed cake. Stir in a pinch of flaky sea salt to each bowl and let cool.

Preheat the oven to 350°F (180°C). Grease an 8 x 12-inch (21 x 31-cm) deep baking pan and line with parchment paper, leaving a few inches overhang on each side.

To make the cake, melt the butter, molasses, corn syrup, stem ginger syrup and vanilla in a small saucepan. Once the butter has melted, remove from the heat and stir in the sugar to dissolve. Let it cool slightly for a few minutes. In a medium bowl, whisk together the eggs and milk and pour this into the butter/sugar mixture. Sift the flour, baking soda, ginger, cinnamon and cloves into the batter and beat briefly to fully combine. Pour the batter into the prepared pan and bake for 40 to 45 minutes, or until the cake is well risen and a toothpick inserted into the center comes out clean. Let the cake cool completely before removing from the pan.

(Continued)

FOR THE BUTTERCREAM

²/₃ cup (150 g) butter

1½ cups (200 g) confectioners' sugar

1-2 tbsp (15-30 ml) milk, if needed

To make the buttercream, beat the butter in a stand mixer or with an electric whisk for 3 minutes, or until pale and creamy. Add the sugar and beat for 5 minutes, or until the buttercream is thick and fluffy. Take the bowl that had two-thirds of the melted chocolate and pour this into the buttercream, beating for 1 minute until combined. If the chocolate has solidified, add it back to the oven for a few minutes to melt again. If the buttercream looks too stiff, stir in 1 to 2 tablespoons (15 to 30 ml) of milk to loosen. When the cake is completely cool, spread the buttercream evenly on top going all the way to the edge. Drizzle on the rest of the melted chocolate in a random fashion before serving.

Tips: Make sure to use a white chocolate with at least 30 to 35 percent cocoa solids. Anything less won't give you the right results. If you can't locate stem ginger syrup, replace with 1 tablespoon (15 ml) of corn or golden syrup.

CITRUS

For me, the beauty of citrus lies in its versatility and ability to blend seamlessly into all seasons of the year. Despite the fact that most citrus fruits are at their best in winter here in the U.K., I often associate the bright zing of lemons with spring and summer, when its initial tartness softens to a sweet lightness that sings on your lips. Clementines at Christmas provide a much-needed pop of orange to cut through the gloomy winter days, whereas limes feel inherently tropical, possessing the ability to instantly transport you to a sandy beach.

In this chapter, I want to get us all out of the rut of just sticking to the classics. Now, I am a sucker for a good lemon drizzle cake and have never been known to turn a slice down, but as much of a faithful crowd-pleaser as it is, there is so much more that can be done with it to make it that little bit more intriguing or unexpected. Substituting in some ground pistachios and almonds with a bit of cardamom into my Pistachio, Cardamom & Lemon Drizzle Cake (page 97) brings such a welcome fragrance and newness that I think you'll love. My Limoncello & Toasted Meringue Cake (page 93) gives a much more grown-up feel to the palate while still remaining playful with the marshmallow-like topping. Grapefruits, which are notorious for their intense sourness, often get left behind when it comes to baking, but I've given it a new lease on life in my Double Ginger & Grapefruit Cakes (page 100) with a silky grapefruit curd.

In this chapter, we'll be infusing citrus flavors through syrups, zests and glazes, each bringing a different layer of flavor to each cake. The zest is the bright outer skin of the fruit that holds in all those fragrant citrus oils, so do use unwaxed fruit if you're able to. I also recommend using a microplane, as they're able to give you a really fine zest. Underneath the zest lies the white pith, which is more often than not discarded because of its bitterness. In cakes where we use the whole fruit, such as the Clementine Cake (page 103), the bitterness isn't overpowering and helps to balance some of the sweetness. The recipes in this chapter will give you the tools to enjoy citrus in a new way.

ORANGE BLOSSOM & YOGURT BUNDT

FOR THE SYRUP

½ cup (100 g) granulated sugar

Juice of 1 orange

FOR THE CAKE

2¼ cups (280 g) all-purpose flour

¾ tsp baking soda

¼ tsp baking powder

½ tsp salt

1 cup plus 2 tbsp (225 g) superfine/
caster sugar

Zest of 2 large oranges

3 eggs

2 tsp (10 ml) orange blossom water

½ tsp vanilla extract

¾ cup (180 ml) olive oil

Scant ⅔ cup (150 ml) yogurt, room
temperature

FOR THE GLAZE

¾ cup (100 g) confectioners' sugar

½ tsp orange blossom water

Juice of ½ orange

You can't go too wrong with a Bundt cake, as the pan does most of the work in making it look stunning with little effort on your part. The orange blossom water adds a perfumed essence without being overpowering and is pleasantly bitter against the sweet orange zest and tangy glaze. This cake keeps exceptionally well; it's doused in syrup to keep the cake moist for days. This would usually be something I might make as a mid-week bake, and it'll be just as good, if not slightly better for a slice on Saturday morning.

YIELD: 12–16 SERVINGS

Preheat the oven to 350°F (180°C). Generously grease a 10-cup (2.6-L) Bundt pan with some butter and dust lightly with flour, tapping out the excess. Be sure to get into all the nooks and crannies to make sure the cake doesn't stick when baked.

To make the syrup, heat the sugar and orange juice in a small saucepan until the sugar dissolves. Set aside.

To make the cake, sift together the flour, baking soda, baking powder and salt in a medium bowl. Set aside. In a large bowl, add the sugar and orange zest. Rub the zest in the sugar with your fingertips until it resembles wet sand. Add the eggs, orange blossom water and vanilla and using a stand mixer or electric whisk, beat on medium-high speed for 3 to 5 minutes, or until the eggs are thick and pale. Turn the mixer to a low speed and alternate adding the dry ingredients and the olive oil. Stir in the yogurt before pouring the batter into the Bundt pan and bake for 30 to 40 minutes, or until a toothpick inserted in the center comes out clean.

Poke plenty of holes across the top of the cake with a toothpick. Pour the syrup on top, letting it seep through the holes. Let the cake cool for exactly 10 minutes before inverting it onto a wire rack to cool completely. If you try to remove the cake from the pan too early or too late, it could stick to the pan.

To make the glaze, mix the sugar and orange blossom water in a small bowl. Add the orange juice 1 spoonful at a time until you have a smooth, pourable consistency. If it's too thin, add a little more sugar, and if it's too thick, add a little more orange juice or water. Pour the glaze evenly over the cake and serve.

LIMONCELLO & TOASTED MERINGUE CAKE

Holidays in Italy with my family always meant a chilled limoncello digestif after our meal. If I could bottle up summer and take it with me wherever I went, there would be plenty of limoncello involved. I like to think of this as a refreshingly grown-up lemon drizzle that is still young at heart. The billowy Italian meringue ensures it doesn't take itself too seriously.

YIELD: 1 SQUARE 9-INCH (23-CM) CAKE

FOR THE CAKE

4 eggs

1½ cups (300 g) superfine/caster sugar

½ cup (120 ml) vegetable or sunflower oil

2 cups (250 g) all-purpose flour

1 tbsp (15 g) baking powder

¼ tsp salt

½ cup (120 ml) milk, room temperature

Zest of 2 lemons

Juice of 1 lemon

2 tbsp (30 ml) limoncello

FOR THE SYRUP

¼ cup (50 g) granulated sugar

2 tbsp (30 ml) limoncello

¼ cup (60 ml) water

FOR THE MERINGUE

1 cup (200 g) superfine/caster sugar

3 tbsp (45 ml) water

Scant ½ cup (100 g) egg whites, room temperature

Tip: To create a more intricate topping, spoon the meringue into a piping bag fitted with an open or closed star nozzle. Pipe swirls or roses on top of the cake before blowtorching.

Preheat the oven to 350°F (180°C). Grease a deep 9 x 9-inch (23 x 23-cm) cake pan and line the bottom with parchment paper.

To make the cake, beat the eggs and sugar using a stand mixer or electric whisk for 3 to 5 minutes, or until thick and pale. With the mixer still running, slowly pour in the oil. Stir in the flour, baking powder and salt followed by the milk and lemon zest. Beat until smooth before stirring in the lemon juice and limoncello. Pour the batter into the prepared pan and bake for 35 to 40 minutes, or until well risen and a toothpick inserted into the center comes out clean. Let the cake cool for 10 minutes before turning it out onto a wire rack to cool completely.

To make the syrup, heat the sugar, limoncello and water together in a small saucepan until the sugar dissolves. Prick the surface of the cake with a toothpick and pour on the syrup, letting it seep through.

To make the meringue, add the sugar and water to a medium saucepan and bring to a boil, swirling the pan to dissolve the sugar. Once it reaches a boil, do not stir, as the syrup may crystallize. Heat the sugar until it reaches a temperature of 238°F (115°C). Before adding the egg whites to the bowl of a stand mixer, make sure there is absolutely no trace of grease, or the egg whites won't get stiff. I like to wipe the bowl with a lemon wedge just to be safe. Whip the egg whites on low speed for 1 minute, or until foamy. Increase the speed to medium and whip for 2 to 4 minutes, or until you have soft peaks. To check for soft peaks, pull the mixer head out of the bowl. It should form peaks that fall back onto themselves quite quickly.

Once the sugar has reached the right temperature and with the mixer still running, slowly pour the syrup down the side of the bowl, taking care not to pour the syrup onto the beaters. The sugar will be extremely hot so be very careful. Continue to whip the meringue on high speed until you have thick, glossy, stiff peaks and the bowl is cool to the touch.

Spoon the meringue on top of the cooled cake, leaving about a ½ inch (1.3 cm) from the edge. Use a blowtorch to lightly toast the meringue. If you don't have a blowtorch, you could place the cake under a grill or broiler for a minute or two. Keep a close eye on it, as the meringue will brown very quickly.

LIME, COCONUT & MANGO LAMINGTONS

Some of my favorite brunch spots in London are run by Australians and that's where I had my first lamington. My own spin on the Australian classic injects zesty limes and sweet ripe mangoes, taking me right to the beach. For minimal effort, you can make the sponge a day in advance before dipping and rolling on the day you want to serve. To fully immerse yourself into character and feel like you're living the island life, serve these with cream that's been whipped with a splash of white rum.

YIELD: 16 LAMINGTONS

FOR THE CAKE

1½ cups (190 g) all-purpose flour

1½ tbsp (12 g) cornstarch

1 tbsp (15 g) baking powder

Zest of 2 limes

1 cup (200 g) superfine/caster sugar

1 cup (225 g) unsalted butter

1 tsp vanilla extract

3 eggs

½ cup (120 ml) milk

FOR THE PUREE

2 medium, ripe mangoes

¾ cup (105 g) confectioners' sugar

Juice of 1 lime

2 cups (200 g) desiccated or shredded unsweetened coconut

Preheat the oven to 350°F (180°C). Grease a deep 8 x 12-inch (21 x 31-cm) baking pan and line with parchment paper, leaving an approximately 1-inch (2.5-cm) overhang on all sides.

To make the cake, sift together the flour, cornstarch and baking powder in a medium bowl and set aside. Place the lime zest and sugar in the bowl of a stand mixer or a large mixing bowl. Rub the zest into the sugar with your fingertips until it resembles wet sand. Add the butter and vanilla and beat for 3 to 5 minutes, or until pale and fluffy. Add the eggs, one at a time, beating well after each addition. Mix in the flour and milk in alternate batches, starting and ending with the flour. Pour the batter into the prepared pan and bake for 30 to 40 minutes, or until a toothpick inserted into the center comes out clean.

To make the puree, peel and roughly chop the mangoes and transfer the pieces into a food processor or blender with the sugar and lime juice. Process until smooth and then pour into a shallow-but-wide dish.

Once the cake is completely cool, trim the edges with a sharp knife and cut the cake into 16 even cubes. Dip each square of cake into the mango puree, making sure all sides have been coated, and then roll it in the coconut. Place on a wire rack to firm up and continue with all the cakes.

PISTACHIO, CARDAMOM & LEMON DRIZZLE CAKE

This has to be one of my all-time favorite cakes. This is the one I turn to when I don't have time to think up something new but I know will be a real crowd-pleaser. My mum is also a fan of this and will ask me to make this for her at every opportunity. It holds quite a few special memories; namely, it's the very first cake I baked in the *Bake Off* tent. It's been improved on a little since then but still has all the charm and flavor that made me love it in the first place: creamy pistachios intertwined with fragrant citrusy cardamom and drizzled with a tangy lemon syrup and glaze. If there's only one cake you bake from this book, I won't be mad if it's this one.

YIELD: SERVES 6-8

FOR THE LOAF

1¼ cups (150 g) shelled pistachios, plus extra to decorate

¾ cup plus 1 tbsp (190 ml) vegetable or sunflower oil

Scant 1 cup (190 g) superfine/caster sugar

3 eggs

1½ tsp (8 g) vanilla bean paste

12 green cardamom pods, seeds removed and ground (to make 1½ tsp [3 g] ground cardamom)

Zest of 1 lemon

1½ cups (190 g) all-purpose flour

½ cup (45 g) ground almonds

Pinch of salt

1½ tsp (8 g) baking powder

1 tsp baking soda

⅓ cup (75 ml) sour cream

FOR THE SYRUP

Juice of 3 lemons

½ cup (100 g) superfine/caster sugar

¼ tsp ground cardamom

FOR THE GLAZE

⅔ cup (80 g) confectioners' sugar

1-2 tbsp (15-30 ml) lemon juice

Preheat the oven to 350°F (180°C). Grease a 2-pound (900-g) loaf pan and line with parchment paper.

To make the loaf, pulse the pistachios a few times in a food processor to make a coarse powder and set aside. In a large bowl, mix the oil and sugar. Add the eggs, vanilla paste, ground cardamom and lemon zest. Stir until combined. In a medium bowl, add the flour, ground pistachios, almonds, salt, baking powder and baking soda. Stir until well combined and then fold this into the wet ingredients. Fold in the sour cream. Pour the mixture into the prepared pan and bake for 45 to 50 minutes, or until a toothpick inserted into the middle of the cake comes out clean.

To make the syrup, heat the lemon juice, sugar and cardamom in a saucepan until the sugar is dissolved, then briefly bring to a boil. Remove from the heat and set aside. As soon as the cake is out of the oven, poke holes all over the top with a toothpick. Pour the hot syrup over the cake and leave to cool in the pan for 5 to 10 minutes before turning it out onto a wire rack to cool completely.

For the lemon glaze, sift the sugar into a bowl and stir in the lemon juice until smooth. Drizzle over the cooled cake. If you want a thicker drizzle, add a little more sugar. Finely chop the remaining pistachios and scatter them over the cake.

BLOOD ORANGE & OLIVE OIL UPSIDE— DOWN CAKE

⅓ cup (75 g) light brown sugar

1 tbsp (15 ml) water

2 blood oranges, divided

¾ cup (150 g) superfine/caster sugar

⅓ cup (90 ml) plain yogurt

2 eggs

3 tbsp (45 ml) extra-virgin olive oil

1⅓ cups (165 g) all-purpose flour

1 tsp baking powder

¼ tsp baking soda

Pinch of salt

Every winter without fail, I become obsessed with the dramatic flair of the blood orange. They arrive in the new year like a Christmas gift that got lost in the mail, and before you can blink, there's an influx of blood orange everything, everywhere. The crimson flesh is not as sweet as a regular orange, and it is a little tarter. Using these in an upside-down cake really shows them off in all their glory and are contrasted by the slight peppery edge from the olive oil.

YIELD: 1 ROUND 9-INCH (23-CM) CAKE

Preheat the oven to 350°F (180°C). Grease a round, loose-bottomed 9-inch (23-cm) cake pan and line the bottom with parchment paper.

In a small bowl, mix the brown sugar and water to make a thick paste. Spread this thinly and evenly onto the base of the cake pan and set aside.

Zest 1 orange and add this to a large bowl with the superfine sugar. Rub the zest into the sugar with your fingertips until the zest is evenly distributed. Set aside.

Slice both oranges as thinly as you can with the skin on and arrange the slices on top of the brown sugar base in the cake pan. You can cut some of the slices in half to create a different pattern and to fill in any large gaps.

Add the yogurt to the bowl with the sugar and whisk briefly to combine. Whisk in the eggs and olive oil. Stir in the flour, baking powder, baking soda and salt until smooth. Gently pour the batter on top of the orange slices, being careful not to disturb the oranges underneath. Bake for 30 to 35 minutes, or until the sponge is firm to the touch and golden brown. Leave the cake in its pan to cool completely before attempting to turn it upside down.

DOUBLE GINGER & GRAPEFRUIT CAKES

FOR THE GRAPEFRUIT CURD

1 cup (240 ml) freshly squeezed grapefruit juice, seeds and pulp strained

1/2 cup (100 g) superfine/caster sugar

Zest of 3 red or pink grapefruit, divided

2 eggs

4 egg yolks

1/3 cup (75 g) unsalted butter, softened

FOR THE CAKES

3/4 cup (180 g) unsalted butter

1 cup (200 g) light brown sugar

1 tbsp (20 ml) corn syrup or golden syrup

3/4 cup (80 g) stem (preserved) ginger, pureed

Zest of 1 red grapefruit

2 eggs, lightly beaten

1/2 cup (120 ml) milk, room temperature

1 1/4 cups (150 g) all-purpose flour

2 tsp (10 g) baking soda

2 tbsp (10 g) ground ginger

I only ever eat grapefruit when it has been put into some sort of baked good. I would love to say that my palate was refined enough to enjoy them as they come, but I much prefer them balanced with a little sugar and spice yet still maintaining that distinctive sourness through the sharp curd that gets swirled into the creamy buttercream. There's also plenty of ginger going on in these cakes—both ground and pureed stem, or preserved, ginger that gives a real warm depth of flavor.

YIELD: 12 CAKES

To make the curd, simmer the grapefruit juice in a medium saucepan and let it reduce to about 1/2 cup (120 ml). Leave to cool slightly.

In a heatproof bowl, add the sugar and grapefruit zest. Reserve a few spoonfuls of zest for decorating the cakes. Rub the zest into the sugar with your fingertips until it feels like moist sand. Whisk in the eggs and yolks until fully combined, and then add the butter and cooled grapefruit juice. Pour the mixture into the saucepan and whisk constantly for 5 to 10 minutes, or until the butter has melted and the curd has thickened enough to coat the back of a spoon. Transfer the curd to a bowl and cover with plastic wrap that touches the surface of the curd. Let it cool to room temperature before chilling it in the fridge.

To make the cakes, preheat the oven to 350°F (180°C). Grease the inside of a 12-hole friand tray, dust lightly with flour and tap out the excess. Melt the butter, sugar and corn syrup in a medium saucepan over medium heat, and stir to dissolve the sugar without letting it come to a boil. Remove from the heat and allow it to cool for a few minutes before stirring in the pureed stem ginger and grapefruit zest. Pour the mixture into a large bowl and whisk in the eggs and milk.

Sift the flour, baking soda and ground ginger on top before mixing to get a smooth batter. Fill each friand hole three-quarters of the way up and bake in the oven for 22 to 28 minutes, or until a toothpick inserted into the center comes out clean. Let them cool in the tray for 10 minutes before turning them out onto a wire rack to cool completely.

²/₃ cup (150 g) unsalted butter, softened

2¹/₂ cups (300 g) confectioners' sugar

1 tsp vanilla extract

1 tbsp (15 ml) milk

To make the buttercream, beat the butter and sugar using a stand mixer or electric whisk for 3 to 5 minutes, or until pale and creamy. Add the vanilla extract and milk and beat for 2 minutes, or until smooth. Stir in roughly 3 tablespoons (45 g) of the grapefruit curd. Transfer the buttercream to a piping bag fitted with a nozzle of your choice. Pipe some buttercream onto the center of the cake and spoon a little grapefruit curd on top followed by a sprinkle of grated grapefruit zest.

*See photo on page 9.

Tips: You could make these larger or smaller by using a mini-cupcake tray or a muffin pan. Using different nozzles in the piping bag can help achieve different looks. Try a plain, round nozzle for something more understated or glide a petal tip from left to right to create a ruffle effect. If you can't find stem ginger, you can use finely chopped, crystalized ginger instead.

CLEMENTINE CAKE

FOR THE PUREE

6 clementines

FOR THE CAKE

6 eggs

1¼ cups plus 2 tbsp (275 g)
superfine/caster sugar

1½ cups (150 g) ground almonds

½ cup (85 g) polenta/coarse
cornmeal

1 tsp baking powder

¼ tsp ground ginger

Confectioners' sugar, to dust

Crème fraîche, to serve

Don't be fooled by the unassuming appearance of this cake. What it lacks in height or extravagance is more than made up for in flavor. If you're a fan of marmalade, then this cake is especially for you. Whole clementines are boiled until soft before being blitzed—skin and all—to a puree. It's got just the right balance of bitterness and sweetness and is so incredibly moist without the need to be soaked in syrup. I will say that it does taste better the next day once the flavors have had a chance to settle in, but if you're like me, it may not last that long. A simple dollop of crème fraîche is all that's required to make this the perfect end to a dinner with friends.

YIELD: 1 ROUND 9-INCH (23-CM) CAKE

Preheat the oven to 375°F (190°C). Grease a round 9-inch (23-cm) cake pan and line the bottom with parchment paper.

To make the puree, place the clementines in a saucepan of water and bring to a boil, and then simmer for 20 minutes. Drain the water out and cover the clementines with fresh water. This helps to get rid of some of the bitterness. Bring the water to a boil and then simmer again for 30 minutes, or until the clementines have softened and are squishy to the touch. Drain and leave to cool for 10 minutes. Once cooled, cut them into quarters and remove any pips. Place the clementines, including the skin, in a food processor or blender and pulse until smooth. You should have approximately 1½ cups (350 g) of puree. This step can be done ahead with the puree stored in the fridge for up to 2 days.

To make the cake, use a stand mixer fitted with the whisk attachment or an electric mixer to whisk the eggs and sugar for 2 to 3 minutes, or until thick and pale. Fold in the clementine puree. Gently stir in the almonds, polenta, baking powder and ground ginger. Pour the batter into the prepared cake pan and bake for 45 to 55 minutes, or until a toothpick inserted in the center comes out clean. This cake can brown quite quickly so if it gets too dark, cover it with a sheet of foil and continue to bake. Leave it in the pan to cool completely before removing and dusting with confectioners' sugar. Serve with a spoonful of crème fraîche.

LEMON, RICOTTA & THYME MINI–LOAVES

FOR THE LOAVES

1 cup (200 g) superfine/caster sugar

Zest of 2 lemons

1 tbsp (8 g) finely chopped fresh thyme

½ cup (120 ml) sunflower or vegetable oil

1 cup (250 g) ricotta

2 eggs

1½ cups (190 g) all-purpose flour

2 tsp (10 g) baking powder

Pinch of salt

FOR THE ICING

1¼ cups (150 g) confectioners' sugar

Juice of 1 lemon

8 fresh thyme sprigs

Lemon and thyme is a pairing that I've loved for quite some time. Having been proven to work well together in savory foods, I saw no reason why they couldn't be used in a sweeter setting. The bright, zingy lemon contrasts the aromatic undertones of the fresh thyme sprigs but neither gets lost in the other. The ricotta brings a creamier, richer texture and cuts through some of the lemon's sharpness.

YIELD: 8 MINI–LOAVES

Preheat the oven to 350°F (180°C). Grease eight mini-loaf pans and line each bottom with a strip of parchment paper.

To make the loaves, place the sugar and zest into a large bowl. Using your fingertips, rub the zest into the sugar. This helps to release some essential oils for a more intense fragrance. Stir in the thyme. Add the oil, ricotta and eggs and whisk until smooth. Gently stir in the flour, baking powder and salt and divide the batter evenly into the prepared pans. Bake for 27 to 30 minutes, or until the loaves are lightly golden and a toothpick inserted in the center comes out clean. Leave to cool for a few minutes in the pans before turning them out onto a wire rack to cool completely.

To make the icing, add the sugar to a medium bowl and add enough lemon juice to make a thick-but-pourable glaze. If the glaze becomes too runny, mix in more sugar. Equally, if you think it's too thick to pour, add a little more lemon juice. Spoon the glaze onto the cakes, letting it drip over the edges, and top with a sprig of thyme.

CITRUS POPPY SEED CAKE

1½ cups (190 g) all-purpose flour

Pinch of salt

2 tsp (10 g) baking powder

1 cup (200 g) superfine/caster sugar

Zest of 1 orange, 1 white grapefruit and 2 lemons

¾ cup plus 1 tbsp (190 g) unsalted butter, room temperature

3 eggs

2 tbsp (30 ml) sour cream

2 tbsp (18 g) poppy seeds

FOR THE GLAZE

1¼ cups (150 g) confectioners' sugar

Juice of ½ white grapefruit and ½ orange

Zest of grapefruit, orange or lemon, to decorate

What's a chapter on citrus without a citrus cake! This is a little celebration of the sweetness, tartness and zingy-ness of these much-loved fruits. More than anything, I love the flexibility of this cake. If I'm all out of lemons, then I'll double up on the grapefruit or orange and maybe even throw in a lime. There's plenty of room to play around with the proportions of zest and juice to suit your own tastes or to use up a glut. When I want something bright and refreshing with a homey feel, this is the cake I'm going for. It's the sort of thing you'd want to casually have on hand for unexpected visitors.

YIELD: 8 SERVINGS

Preheat the oven to 325°F (170°C). Grease a 2-pound (900-g) loaf pan and line the bottom with parchment paper.

To make the cake, sift together the flour, salt and baking powder in a medium bowl and set aside. Add the sugar and zests to the bowl of a stand mixer. Rub the zest into the sugar using your fingertips until it resembles wet sand. Add the butter and beat on medium-high speed for 3 to 5 minutes, or until pale and creamy. Add the eggs one at a time, beating well after each addition. If the mixture looks like it is starting to curdle, add 1 tablespoon (8 g) of the flour mixture. Turn the mixer down to low and add the flour mixture. Once incorporated, stir in the sour cream followed by the poppy seeds, making sure they are evenly distributed. Pour the batter into the prepared cake pan and bake for 40 to 45 minutes, or until a toothpick inserted in the center comes out clean.

To make the glaze, mix together the sugar and citrus juice in a small bowl. Once the cake is out of the oven, use a toothpick to poke holes across the cake going all the way down. Spoon the glaze evenly over the cake, letting it soak through the holes before adding more. Let it cool completely before removing from the pan. Top with some shaved citrus zest.

FLORAL

A gift of fresh flowers can instantly brighten up my day. Every so often, my mum will buy flowers for the house, and as soon as you walk into the room, you can't help but notice how much life they bring to their surroundings. Whatever I'm doing in that moment, I'll pause to just take in their beauty, inhale the scents and somehow my day would be all the better for it. That same feeling comes when I bake or decorate cakes with fresh flowers and floral flavors.

From rose petals to elderflower to jasmine blossoms, there's a delicacy and elegance that's quite refreshing. To me, the cakes in this chapter feel like springtime, bringing promises of new buds and blossoms. The very best of nature's color palette is shown off in these recipes, from the deep purple hibiscus flowers to the dusky yellow chamomile and the beautiful array of colors in The Wedding Cake (page 113). When it comes to styling, using fresh flowers brings such a youthful and modern feel—the flowers do all the work so you can keep everything else quite simple and pared back, leaving you with a cake that is stunning to look at.

As well as decorating with both edible and decorative flowers, recipes such as the Coconut, Raspberry & Rose Roulade (page 127) incorporate floral flavors with ingredients such as rosewater. I use both dried rose petals and rosewater quite a bit in my baking—partly from my love of Middle Eastern cuisine but also because of the alluring perfumed edge that it imparts. A little goes a long way with rosewater, and different brands will vary in strength, so do be careful with how much you use. Start small and increase to taste. Honey is also a fantastic way to introduce flowery elements that add subtle complexities in flavor. I often go for an orange blossom honey as used in the Honey Loaf with Sweet Dukkah (page 123), but a good lavender honey is also a favorite.

ELDERFLOWER & ROASTED STRAWBERRY LAYER CAKE

FOR THE CAKE

Scant 2 cups (230 g) all-purpose flour

2½ tsp (11 g) baking powder

3 tbsp (45 ml) milk

2 tbsp (30 ml) elderflower cordial

1 cup (225 g) unsalted butter

1 cup plus 2 tbsp (230 g) superfine/caster sugar

Zest of 1 lemon

4 eggs

FOR THE PUREE

Approximately 1 lb (400–450 g) fresh strawberries

¼ cup (50 g) superfine/caster sugar

2 tsp (10 g) vanilla bean paste

This is quite the celebration cake and is my go-to when I want a summery showstopper. Roasting the strawberries is a real game-changer and brings out such an intense, sweet flavor, it's well worth the extra step. When the roasted strawberry puree merges into the Swiss meringue buttercream, it creates a creamy flavor reminiscent of strawberry ice cream. Swiss meringue buttercream requires a few more steps than a classic buttercream but has a much lighter and silkier texture and carries the strawberry flavor exceptionally well. As it is quite an involved cake, you can make the strawberries and cake layers in advance and then prepare the buttercream on the day you will assemble.

YIELD: 1 ROUND 6-INCH (15-CM) LAYER CAKE

Preheat the oven to 350°F (180°C). Grease the base and sides of three deep, round 6-inch (15-cm) cake pans and line the bottoms with parchment paper.

To make the cake, sift together the flour and baking powder in a large bowl, and set aside. Mix the milk and elderflower cordial in a small bowl and set aside. Using a stand mixer or electric whisk, beat the butter, sugar and lemon zest for 5 minutes, or until pale and fluffy. Add the eggs one at a time, beating well after each addition. If the mixture looks like it's starting to curdle, add 1 tablespoon (8 g) of the flour mixture. Turn the mixer speed to low and add half of the flour mixture followed by the milk and elderflower. Stir in the remaining flour and divide the batter equally into the prepared cake pans. Bake the cakes for 35 to 37 minutes, or until a toothpick inserted in the center comes out clean. Let the cakes cool in their pans for 10 minutes before turning them out onto a wire rack to cool completely. Once cool, wrap them tightly in plastic wrap and place in the fridge to firm up.

To make the puree, preheat the oven to 375°F (190°C). Slice the stems off the strawberries, cut them in half and put them into a baking dish. Toss the fruit with the sugar and vanilla. Roast the strawberries in the oven for 30 to 40 minutes, stirring once halfway. The strawberries are done once they are soft and fragrant and the juices have turned into a syrup. Leave the strawberries to cool completely before transferring them to a food processor or blender and pulsing until smooth. Store in an airtight container in the fridge until you're ready to use it.

(Continued)

ELDERFLOWER & ROASTED STRAWBERRY LAYER CAKE (CONTINUED)

FOR THE BUTTERCREAM

$^{1}/_{2}$ cup plus 1 tbsp (150 g) egg whites

1 cup (200 g) superfine/caster sugar

$1^{1}/_{3}$ cups (300 g) unsalted butter, softened

FOR ASSEMBLY AND DECORATING

6 tbsp (90 ml) elderflower cordial

Fresh strawberries, to decorate

Fresh elderflower, to decorate

Tip: When making layer cakes, a turntable comes in very handy for decorating, making it easier for you to get an even layer of buttercream all around the cake. The trick is to turn the turntable slowly with one hand while using a bench scraper or palette knife in the other.

To make the buttercream, add the egg whites and sugar to the bowl of a stand mixer or a heatproof bowl. Make sure there are no traces of grease in the bowl as this will stop the meringue from whipping up. Place the bowl over a saucepan of simmering water, making sure that the base doesn't touch the water. Whisk the eggs and sugar constantly until the mixture reaches a temperature of about 150°F (65°C). If you don't have a thermometer, rub a little of the mixture in between your fingers. The eggs should be hot to the touch with all the sugar dissolved.

Remove the bowl from the heat and start whisking the egg whites on high speed in a stand mixer fitted with the whisk attachment or with an electric whisk. Beat until the whites are thick and have doubled in volume. Once the bowl is cool to the touch and with the mixer still running, add the butter a piece at a time. The meringue will deflate and will start to look a little runny or curdled. Don't panic—this is normal. Continue beating until you have added in all of the butter and the mixture is smooth and glossy. If after 10 minutes, your meringue buttercream is still soupy, chill it in the fridge for 20 minutes and then beat again. Add about $^{1}/_{2}$ cup (125 g) of the strawberry puree and beat the buttercream for 2 minutes, or until smooth. Leave the buttercream at room temperature until you are ready to assemble.

Unwrap the cakes from the fridge and if any of them are domed, level them with a serrated knife or a cake leveler. All the layers need to be completely flat to ensure you don't end up with a wonky cake. Brush each cake layer with 2 tablespoons (30 ml) of elderflower cordial. Place one layer of cake on a cake board and put this board on a turntable, if using. If your buttercream has firmed up, whip it up again in the mixer until smooth. Add a scoop of buttercream and spread it out evenly with an offset spatula, pushing the buttercream right to the edge (it's fine if it spills over). Place the next layer on top of the first, but this time add about 1 tablespoon (8 g) of strawberry puree on top of the buttercream layer, leaving about 1 inch (2.5 cm) clear around the edge. Place the last layer topside down to give you a perfectly flat top.

Frost the top and sides of the cake with a thin layer of buttercream. Smooth the edges as much as you can with a bench scraper or palette knife. This is the crumb coat layer that will trap any stray crumbs and act as a base for the next layer. Place the cake in the fridge for 20 minutes to firm up before adding another layer of buttercream on the top and sides. Fill a piping bag fitted with an open star nozzle (I've used Wilton 8B) with any remaining buttercream and pipe swirls across the edge to make a wreath. Top the cake with fresh strawberries, a drizzle of any leftover puree and fresh elderflower (if in season).

THE WEDDING CAKE

3¹/₂ cups (450 g) all-purpose flour

3¹/₂ tsp (18 g) baking powder

¹/₂ tsp baking soda

¹/₄ tsp salt

1¹/₄ cups (285 g) unsalted butter

1³/₄ cups plus 1 tbsp (375 g) superfine/caster sugar

5 eggs

Scant 1 cup (225 ml) buttermilk

1 tbsp (15 g) vanilla bean paste

FOR THE JAM

2¹/₂ cups (300 g) fresh raspberries

1¹/₂ cups (300 g) superfine/caster sugar

¹/₂ tbsp (8 ml) lemon juice

1¹/₂ tsp (8 ml) orange blossom water

Every year, I make a birthday cake for myself and my twin sister. Sometimes, I'll ask what she wants, but most of the time I have full creative control to make whatever I fancy. Last year, I went all out and made a little two-tiered cake decorated with fresh flowers—it was stunning. Upon seeing it, her first response was, "Why did you make us a wedding cake?" And that's how it got its name! This is my sister's favorite cake with layers of vanilla buttermilk sponge sandwiched together with a floral raspberry and orange blossom jam. It could definitely make a cute wedding cake, or if you're just a little extra like me, it also doubles up as an epic birthday cake. The floral decoration is what makes this cake stand out, and depending on which flowers you use, it can have a different look each time.

YIELD: 16–20 SERVINGS

Preheat the oven to 350°F (180°C). Grease three deep, round 6-inch (15-cm) cake pans and one deep, round 4-inch (10-cm) cake pan and line with parchment paper.

To make the cake, sift together the flour, baking powder, baking soda and salt in a bowl and set aside. Using a stand mixer or electric whisk, beat the butter and sugar for 3 to 5 minutes, or until pale and creamy. Add the eggs one at a time, beating well after each addition and scraping down the sides of the bowl every so often. If the mixture looks like it's starting to curdle, add 1 tablespoon (8 g) of the flour mix. With the mixer still running, turn the speed down to low and pour in half of the flour. Once this is combined, pour in the buttermilk and vanilla, followed by the remaining flour. Beat for a few seconds until you have a smooth batter. Divide the batter between the four pans and bake for 20 to 25 minutes. Check that the 4-inch (10-cm) cake is fully baked and a toothpick inserted into the center comes out clean. Remove it from the oven and continue to bake the other layers for 10 to 15 minutes. Remove the cakes from the oven; let them cool in the pans for 10 minutes before turning them out onto a wire rack to cool completely. Once completely cool, wrap the cakes tightly in plastic wrap and put them in the fridge for at least 45 minutes to firm up before layering.

To make the jam, place a small plate in the freezer to chill. You'll use this later to test if the jam is ready. Add the raspberries, sugar and lemon juice to a deep, medium saucepan. Cook on low heat for 4 to 6 minutes until the sugar has completely dissolved. Bring the fruit to a boil and cook the jam for 3 to 5 minutes. Spoon a little of the jam onto the plate in the freezer. Let it cool for a few minutes and then push your finger into the jam. If it wrinkles, then the jam is ready. If not, cook the jam for 2 minutes and test it again. Once the jam is ready, remove from the heat and stir in the orange blossom water. Transfer to a bowl to cool completely.

(Continued)

FOR THE BUTTERCREAM

1¹/₃ cups (300 g) unsalted butter, softened

4¹/₂ cups (550 g) confectioners' sugar

2 tsp (10 g) vanilla bean paste

3 tbsp (45 ml) warm milk

FOR ASSEMBLY

Fresh flowers and foliage such as eucalyptus, thistles, hydrangeas, pansies and roses

Toothpicks

Flower tape

To make the buttercream, beat the butter using a stand mixer or electric whisk for 3 to 5 minutes, or until pale and creamy. Add the sugar and vanilla and beat for 6 to 8 minutes, or until the buttercream is thick and pale. Beat in the warm milk until smooth and then set aside the buttercream at room temperature until you're ready to assemble.

Unwrap the cakes from the fridge and if any of them are domed, level them with a serrated knife or a cake leveler. All the layers need to be completely flat to ensure you don't end up with a wonky cake. Place one 6-inch (15-cm) cake on a cake board and place the cake board on a turntable, if using. Add a scoop of buttercream to the cake and use an offset spatula to spread it out evenly, pushing the buttercream right to the edge. It's fine if it spills over. Add about 1 tablespoon (10 g) of jam and spread this out, leaving 1 inch (2.5 cm) clear of the edges. Place the next layer on top of the first one and repeat. When you get to the last layer, place the cake topside down to give you a perfectly flat top.

Frost the top and sides of the cake with a thin layer of buttercream. Smooth the edges as much as you can with a bench scraper or palette knife using the turntable to help you. This is the crumb coat layer that will trap any stray crumbs. Place the cake in the fridge for 30 minutes to firm up before adding another layer of buttercream on the top and sides, repeating the smoothing process. Let the cake chill in the fridge.

For the top tier, slice the 4-inch (10-cm) cake in half and sandwich the layers together with buttercream and a little jam. Place the cake on a cake board of the same size and frost the top and sides of the cake with a thin layer of buttercream before placing it in the fridge to chill for 30 minutes. Add another, thicker layer of buttercream to the cake and smooth the top and sides with a bench scraper. Place in the fridge to chill.

When the tiers are completely chilled, remove them from the fridge. Use a large offset spatula to help you lift the top tier onto the bottom tier, shifting it to the center. To arrange the flowers, snip off the stems, leaving about a ¹/₂ inch (1.3 cm). Insert a toothpick into the stem and wrap up where they meet with a little flower tape. This flower can now be inserted into the cake up to the flower tape. Arrange the flowers on the top tier or in a cascading style going across the middle.

EARL GREY & BLUEBERRY TEA CAKES

1/2 cup (120 ml) whole milk

3 Earl Grey tea bags or 4 tsp (6 g) of loose leaf

1 tsp vanilla bean paste

2¼ cups plus 1 tbsp (283 g) all-purpose flour, divided

1 tbsp (15 g) baking powder

1 cup (200 g) superfine/caster sugar

Scant 1 cup (200 g) unsalted butter

3 eggs

1⅓ cups (200 g) blueberries, fresh or frozen

2 tbsp (30 g) granulated or demerara sugar, to top

These are my little modern twists on the classic blueberry muffin. The bursts of blueberries nestled in the bergamot-scented Earl Grey sponge make these tea cakes wonderfully fragrant and delicate and a perfect little breakfast cake. Baking with tea provides an instant way to infuse delicate flavors, so make sure to let the tea bags steep in the milk to let the Earl Grey shine through.

YIELD: 10 SERVINGS

Preheat the oven to 350°F (180°C). Grease ten holes of a cupcake pan lightly with butter and dust lightly with flour, tapping out the excess.

In a small saucepan, add the milk, tea bags and vanilla and heat until just before the milk boils. Remove from the heat and let it steep and cool for 10 to 15 minutes. In a medium bowl, sift together 2¼ cups (275 g) flour and the baking powder and set aside. Using a stand mixer or electric whisk, beat the sugar and butter until pale and creamy. Add the eggs one at a time, beating well after each addition. Mix in half of the flour, beating briefly until combined, followed by the milk and remaining flour.

Toss the blueberries in the remaining tablespoon (8 g) of flour, making sure they're evenly coated. This will help to prevent them from sinking to the bottom of the batter. Fold the blueberries gently into the batter, being careful not to break any of them. Divide the batter evenly between the cupcake pan, sprinkle the tops with demerara sugar and bake for 25 to 30 minutes, or until a toothpick inserted into the center comes out clean. A little blueberry juice is fine! Let the cakes cool for 5 minutes in the pans before turning them out onto a wire rack to cool completely.

CHAMOMILE CAKE WITH HONEY CRÈME FRAÎCHE

FOR THE CAKE

1½ cups (190 g) all-purpose flour

½ tbsp (8 g) baking powder

½ tsp salt

⅔ cup plus 1 tbsp (180 ml) milk

5 tbsp (25 g) dried chamomile flowers or 6 tea bags, plus more to decorate

2 tsp (10 ml) vanilla extract

½ cup (115 g) unsalted butter

1 cup (200 g) superfine/caster sugar

2 eggs

FOR THE CRÈME FRAÎCHE

¾ cup (200 ml) crème fraîche

2 tbsp (30 ml) honey

If this cake were a person, it would be someone who appeared rather demure at first glance but within a few minutes would open up to reveal an exuberance that you couldn't help but want to be around. Deftly flavored with soothing chamomile and not overly sweet, it's a cake that I can never just have one slice of, and I find that it's the perfect addition to the table for a spring brunch with the girls. Use a good-quality, whole-flower chamomile for a more potent, aromatic flavor.

YIELD: 8–10 SERVINGS

Preheat the oven to 350°F (180°C). Grease two round 8-inch (20-cm) cake pans and line with parchment paper.

To make the cake, sift together the flour, baking powder and salt in a medium bowl and set aside. In a small saucepan, heat the milk, chamomile and vanilla and simmer for 3 to 5 minutes, or until the milk is hot to the touch but not boiling. Remove from the heat, cover and let the milk steep and cool for 20 minutes. Once cool, strain the flowers or discard the tea bags. Using a stand mixer or electric whisk, beat the butter and sugar together until pale and fluffy. Add the eggs one at a time, beating well after each addition. Add half of the flour and beat briefly until just combined. Pour in the milk, followed by the rest of the flour and beat for a few seconds until you have a smooth batter.

Divide the batter evenly between the prepared pans and bake for 20 to 25 minutes, or until a toothpick inserted into the center comes out clean. Let the cakes cool for 10 minutes before turning them out onto a wire rack to cool completely.

To make the crème fraîche, whisk the crème fraîche and honey together in a bowl for 1 minute, or until it thickens to soft peaks. Sandwich the cakes together with a thin layer of crème fraîche and add a thicker layer on top. Sprinkle some dried chamomile flowers on top, if using.

HIBISCUS BUTTERMILK CAKES

FOR THE CAKES

2½ cups (300 g) all-purpose flour

2 tsp (10 g) baking powder

¼ tsp salt

¾ cup (170 g) unsalted butter

1¼ cups (250 g) superfine/caster sugar

2 tsp (10 g) vanilla bean paste

3 eggs

⅔ cup plus 1 tbsp (180 ml) buttermilk, room temperature

FOR THE HIBISCUS SYRUP

4 tbsp (20 g) dried hibiscus flowers

½ cup plus 1 tbsp (120 g) granulated sugar

½ cup (120 ml) water

FOR THE BUTTERCREAM

1 cup (225 g) unsalted butter, softened

2 cups (270 g) confectioners' sugar

Pinch of salt

2 tbsp (30 ml) milk

3 tbsp (45 ml) Hibiscus Syrup

Dried hibiscus flowers, to decorate

Tip: You can find dried hibiscus flowers online or in some health-food stores.

Whenever I make these cakes, I'm reminded of the novel set in Nigeria called *Purple Hibiscus* by Chimamanda Ngozi Adichie, in which the hibiscus flowers represent freedom and individuality—two things I hope come across well throughout this book. The soft, fluffy buttermilk cakes are simple but so effective in allowing the tangy hibiscus to shine through. I've baked them in a cupcake tray without using cases simply because I prefer the pared-back look it gives, but you could of course use them if you prefer.

YIELD: 12–16 SERVINGS

Preheat the oven to 350°F (180°C). Grease the holes of a regular cupcake tray and dust lightly with flour, tapping out any excess flour.

To make the cake, in a medium bowl, sift together the flour, baking powder and salt and set aside. Beat the butter, sugar and vanilla using a stand mixer or electric whisk for 3 to 5 minutes, or until pale and creamy. Add the eggs one at a time, beating well after each addition. Add half of the flour and beat briefly until combined. Pour in the buttermilk followed by the remaining flour and beat for a few seconds until you have a smooth batter. Pour the batter into each cupcake hole, three-quarters of the way up. Bake for 18 to 25 minutes, or until a toothpick inserted into one of the cakes comes out clean. Let them cool for 5 minutes before turning them out onto a wire rack to cool completely.

To make the syrup, add the dried hibiscus, sugar and water to a small saucepan and bring to a boil. Reduce the heat and simmer for 2 to 3 minutes, or until the syrup starts to thicken a little. Strain the syrup to remove the dried flowers and leave to cool.

To make the buttercream, beat the butter in the bowl of a stand mixer or with an electric whisk for 3 to 5 minutes, or until pale and creamy. Add the sugar and salt and beat for 3 minutes, or until the buttercream is thick and fluffy. Add the milk and beat until combined and then pour in the cooled hibiscus syrup and beat until you have a smooth, pink buttercream. You can add more hibiscus syrup 1 tablespoon (15 ml) at a time until you reach the color you prefer.

Place the buttercream into a disposable piping bag fitted with a plain, round nozzle. Pipe a small blob onto each cake and use the back of a teaspoon or offset spatula to create a little well in the middle. Decorate with either whole, dried hibiscus flowers or pulse them in a food processor to make a powder. If you have any leftover syrup, you could also add a teaspoon into the buttercream wells.

HONEY LOAF WITH SWEET DUKKAH

A crunchy, scented crust protects a soft, honey-soaked sponge in this beautiful loaf. Dukkah is a nutty Egyptian spice mix usually consisting of a variety of herbs, nuts and seeds. The sweeter version used here is a heady blend of fennel, pistachio, rose and coconut that gets smothered on top of the warm honey cake. Using a floral orange blossom honey ties it all together without overpowering, making this a great option for an afternoon treat.

YIELD: SERVES   10–12

Preheat the oven to 375°F (190°C). Grease a 5 x 13-inch (13 x 32-cm) loaf pan and line it with parchment paper, leaving enough overhang on each side to help you pull the cake out once done.

To make the loaf, whisk together in a large bowl the flour, baking powder, baking soda, salt and cinnamon. Make a well in the center and pour in the oil, honey, superfine sugar, brown sugar and eggs and whisk slowly by hand until there are no lumps in the batter. Pour in the vanilla and tea. Continue to stir until the tea is incorporated and the batter is smooth—it will be fairly runny. Pour the batter into the prepared cake pan and bake for 45 to 55 minutes, or until the cake is springy to the touch and a toothpick inserted in the center comes out clean.

To make the syrup, gently heat the honey and water in a small saucepan. Stir until the honey dissolves. Remove from the heat and set aside.

To make the dukkah, place the sesame seeds, fennel seeds, pistachios, cardamom, coconut and rose petals into a spice grinder or food processor and pulse briefly until you have a rough mixture.

Pour the dukkah into the saucepan with the honey syrup and mix to get it all evenly coated. Spread the dukkah evenly on top of the warm cake and leave to cool completely before slicing.

Tip: Play around with the dukkah ingredients to come up with something that is unique to you. It works well with almonds, macadamia nuts and even spices such as coriander and black pepper.

FOR THE LOAF

2¹/₂ cups (300 g) all-purpose flour

1 tsp baking powder

¹/₂ tsp baking soda

Pinch of salt

¹/₂ tsp ground cinnamon

²/₃ cup (160 ml) vegetable or sunflower oil

1 cup (240 ml) orange blossom honey

¹/₂ cup (100 g) superfine/caster sugar

¹/₂ cup (100 g) brown sugar

2 eggs

1 tsp vanilla extract

Scant 1 cup (200 ml) strong-brewed English Breakfast tea

FOR THE SYRUP

3 tbsp (45 ml) honey

¹/₄ cup (60 ml) water

FOR THE DUKKAH

1 tsp white sesame seeds

1 tsp black sesame seeds

1 tsp fennel seeds

4 tbsp (30 g) shelled pistachios

¹/₂ tsp ground cardamom

2 tbsp (15 g) shredded coconut

¹/₂ tsp dried rose petals

JASMINE GREEN TEA CAKE

British people love tea, myself included. Although my mornings will likely start with a black Americano, for the rest of the day I reach for a variety of teas to soothe and refresh. Jasmine green tea is a personal favorite. A light genoise sponge works best here to carry the tea flavor without it getting lost in too rich of a cake. To match the elegance of the jasmine, I've kept the styling really simple.

YIELD: 4 SERVINGS

FOR THE CAKE

¼ cup (60 g) unsalted butter

Leaves from 3 jasmine green tea bags or 1 tbsp (10 g) of loose leaf

4 eggs

²/₃ cup (125 g) superfine/caster sugar

1 cup (125 g) all-purpose flour

FOR THE SYRUP

¼ cup (50 g) superfine/caster sugar

¼ cup (60 ml) water

Zest of 1 lemon

1 tea bag of jasmine green tea

FOR THE GLAZE

²/₃ cup (75 g) confectioners' sugar

2 tbsp (30 ml) water

Preheat the oven to 350°F (180°C). Grease one round 5-inch (13-cm) cake pan and line with parchment paper.

To make the cake, add the butter and the contents of the tea bags to a small saucepan and heat on medium heat until the butter has melted. Remove from the heat and let the tea steep. Add the eggs and sugar to the bowl of a stand mixer or heatproof bowl and set it over a pan of simmering water. Make sure the bottom of the bowl doesn't touch the water. Whisk the eggs until the sugar has dissolved and the mixture is warm to the touch. Remove the bowl from the heat and whisk the eggs with a stand mixer fitted with the whisk attachment or an electric whisk for 4 to 7 minutes, or until the eggs are thick, pale and tripled in volume. To test that the eggs are ready, turn off the mixer, lift out the whisk and let the mixture fall back in. It should leave a trail on the surface that will sink and disappear after a few seconds; this is called the ribbon stage. If this doesn't happen, continue to whisk for 1 minute and repeat.

Sift a third of the flour on top of the eggs and very gently fold it in. You want to be careful not to knock out all of the air you've just incorporated. Sift in the remaining flour and fold again, making sure there are no pockets of flour hiding toward the bottom of the bowl. Carefully remove approximately ½ cup (120 ml) (doesn't need to be exact) of the batter and put it in a small bowl. Pour in the melted green tea butter and stir to thoroughly combine. Fold this butter mixture back into the bowl of batter.

Gently pour the batter into the prepared cake pan and bake for 30 to 36 minutes, or until the cake is well risen and springs back to the touch. Don't open the oven door in the first 20 minutes of baking, as this might cause the cake to sink. Remove the cake from the oven and let it cool for 2 to 3 minutes, and then carefully turn it upside down onto a wire rack while still in the pan to cool completely. This will help avoid any sinking in the middle of the cake.

To make the syrup, add the sugar, water, zest and contents of the tea bag to a small saucepan and heat until the sugar dissolves. Remove the pan from the cake and brush the syrup on top, letting it soak into the cake.

To make the glaze, mix together the sugar and water in a bowl until you have a thick-but-pourable consistency. Pour the icing on top of the cake, letting it spill over the edges.

COCONUT, RASPBERRY & ROSE ROULADE

FOR THE CAKE

1/2 cup (50 g) desiccated or shredded unsweetened coconut

5 eggs

3/4 cup (150 g) superfine/caster sugar

3/4 cup (95 g) all-purpose flour

1/2 tsp baking powder

2 tbsp (30 g) granulated sugar

FOR THE FILLING

1 cup (240 ml) heavy cream

1/4 cup (50 g) superfine/caster sugar

2 tsp (10 ml) vanilla extract

1 2/3 cups (200 g) fresh raspberries

1/2 tsp rosewater

FOR ASSEMBLY

2 tbsp (30 g) desiccated or shredded unsweetened coconut

Confectioners' sugar, to dust

Cakes like these don't last very long. Full of fresh cream and rose-scented raspberries, it might be worth making two of these at a time just so it can last a little longer. The super-light, fatless sponge is studded with desiccated coconut, which also adds a little texture. Once you get the hang of baking and rolling the sponge, you'll soon realize how quick and easy it is to put together.

YIELD: 1 ROULADE

Preheat the oven to 375°F (190°C). Line a 9 x 13-inch (23 x 33-cm) Swiss roll pan with parchment paper.

To make the cake, add the coconut to a food processor and pulse until it's a finer mixture. Using a stand mixer or electric whisk, beat the eggs and superfine sugar for 3 to 5 minutes, or until very pale and doubled in size. Sift the flour, coconut and baking powder on top of the eggs and very gently fold to combine, being careful not to knock out too much air. Gently pour the batter in the prepared pan and bake for 10 to 12 minutes, or until the cake is golden brown and just firm to the touch. If the cake overbakes, it may crack when it comes to rolling.

Place a sheet of parchment paper slightly bigger than the Swiss roll pan onto the countertop and sprinkle liberally with the granulated sugar. Turn the sponge out onto the paper and peel off the paper that was on the bottom of the sponge. Using a sharp knife, score a line about half the cake's depth along one of the shorter edges. Roll the warm cake up tightly in the parchment paper, starting from the side that you scored. Leave the rolled cake to cool completely.

To make the filling, whip the cream in a medium bowl with the sugar and vanilla until you have soft peaks. Slice the raspberries in half and toss them in a bowl with the rosewater. Break the raspberries down a little by lightly pressing with a fork. Stir three-quarters of the raspberries into the cream, allowing the raspberries to create a ripple effect.

Once the sponge is completely cool, gently unroll, and flatten the sponge lightly with your hand. Spread the raspberry filling thickly and evenly across the cake, leaving about a 1/2 inch (1.3 cm) from the edges before sprinkling with the coconut and the remaining raspberries. Reroll the sponge and try to keep as much of the filling inside as possible. Slice off both ends of the cake to reveal the swirl inside. Dust the cake with confectioners' sugar.

Tip: For a completely different look, you can cover the rolled cake in the whipped cream, also covering both ends. Then press on some toasted coconut flakes to cover the entire cake.

FRUIT

When I first started baking, I was always cautious about approaching recipes that used fresh or dried fruits. The thought of baking with fruit would immediately take my mind to a Christmas fruitcake—something I thoroughly disliked and saw as heavy and old-fashioned, crammed with every dried fruit you could imagine and sitting under a cloyingly thick layer of both marzipan and royal icing.

Thankfully, I quickly came to realize that fruitcakes weren't the beginning and end of incorporating fruits into my baking and that actually, it was one of the best things I could do to a cake—they truly are great partners, from the furry skin of a peach, to the curves of a poached pear, from the sticky, wrinkled skin of a date to the sparkling jewels of pomegranate seeds. Fruit is glorious. It adds moisture, texture, flavor and color and is a great way to show off what nature has to offer.

The recipes in this chapter bring a more modern approach to baking with fruit whereby the berries, pomegranates, peaches and more are the focus and not hidden beneath layers of frosting or left to sink to the bottom of the cake. I like to decorate and style my cakes with fresh fruits for an easy eye-catching look in recipes such as the Summer Berry Cake (page 151) or the Fig, Blackberry & Tahini Cake (page 130). The Date & Rooibos Loaf (page 148) is a personal favorite in this chapter because it really reignited a love for dried fruit, which so often gets a bad rap—the sweet dates bring such a concentrated flavor and delightful chewiness that is so irresistible.

Other recipes such as the Sour Cherry & Mahleb Crumble Cake (page 134) let you use either fresh or frozen fruit, meaning you could bake this all year-round. My freezer is always stocked with bags of frozen fruit, as they're incredibly convenient and can add much flexibility to your baking.

FIG, BLACKBERRY & TAHINI CAKE

This cake reminds me of the transitional period in between the end of summer and the arrival of autumn where the air gets cooler, evenings become shorter and I crave something a little more earthy. Both figs with their gooey innards and plump blackberries are at their best around this time, at least in the U.K., and gently usher us into the new season while being just sweet enough to balance the nutty tahini.

YIELD: 8 SERVINGS

FOR THE CAKE

1³/₄ cups (225 g) all-purpose flour

1¹/₂ tsp (8 g) baking powder

Pinch of salt

³/₄ cup plus 2 tbsp (200 g) unsalted butter

Scant 1 cup (200 g) light brown sugar

1 tsp vanilla extract

3 tbsp (60 g) tahini

3 eggs

3 tbsp (50 ml) milk

FOR THE TOPPING

³/₄ cup (160 g) mascarpone

²/₃ cup (80 g) confectioners' sugar

1 tsp vanilla extract

3 tbsp (50 ml) heavy cream

FOR DECORATING

4–6 figs, quartered

A handful of blackberries

1 tsp sesame seeds, lightly toasted

Preheat the oven to 350°F (180°C). Grease a round 9-inch (23-cm) cake pan and line with parchment paper.

To make the cake, sift together the flour, baking powder and salt into a small bowl and set aside. Using a stand mixer or electric whisk, cream together the butter, sugar and vanilla for 5 minutes, or until pale and creamy. Add the tahini and beat for 1 minute, or until combined. Add the eggs one at a time, beating well after each addition and scraping down the bowl every so often. With the mixer on low speed, pour in half of the flour, followed by the milk. Pour in the remainder of the flour and beat gently until combined. Pour the batter into the prepared pan and bake for 30 to 35 minutes, or until the cake is a deep golden brown on top and a toothpick inserted into the center comes out clean. Leave the cake to cool before removing from the pan.

To make the topping, add the mascarpone and confectioners' sugar to a small bowl and mix by hand with a spatula or spoon until smooth. Stir in the vanilla extract and heavy cream to loosen it up before using an offset spatula to spread the mascarpone evenly on top of the cake.

To decorate, arrange the figs and blackberries in a crescent shape along one side of the cake. Finish with a sprinkle of sesame seeds.

PASSIONFRUIT FRIANDS

FOR THE FRIANDS

²/₃ cup (140 g) unsalted butter

Scant ¹/₂ cup (60 g) all-purpose flour

1¹/₄ cups (130 g) ground almonds

1 cup (130 g) confectioners' sugar

4 egg whites

FOR THE TOPPING

Pulp from 2 passionfruits

4 tsp (10 g) confectioners' sugar

These are my tiny bursts of sunshine—moist almond cakes that bake in minutes to give crisp edges with a dense-but-soft interior. Some people prefer to discard the seeds from a passionfruit, but I like the crunch and extra texture they bring. Baking the friands this size has two advantages: they pop in your mouth all in one, meaning it's incredibly easy to eat half a batch without realizing it, but they're also great for serving to a large crowd.

YIELD: 24 MINI-FRIANDS

Preheat the oven to 375°F (190°C). Grease a mini-cupcake pan with melted butter and dust the holes lightly with flour.

To make the friands, add the butter to a saucepan and heat it gently on medium heat for approximately 3 to 4 minutes until the butter turns golden brown and smells sweet and nutty. Transfer to a separate bowl and set aside to cool. In a medium bowl, sift together the flour, almonds and confectioners' sugar and set aside. Froth the egg whites lightly with a fork to break them up and pour into the flour mixture. Fold until combined and then stir in the butter. Spoon the batter into the mini-cupcake pan, filling each hole just below the rim. Bake for 10 to 12 minutes, or until the friands have risen and are springy to the touch.

To make the topping, mix the pulp and sugar in a small bowl and spoon generously onto the cooled cakes.

Tip: These can be baked in a regular-size friand or cupcake pan. Just increase the baking time to 20 to 25 minutes and double the amount of passionfruit topping.

SOUR CHERRY & MAHLEB CRUMBLE CAKE

¼ cup (55 g) unsalted butter, cold

¼ cup (45 g) superfine/caster sugar

⅔ cup (75 g) all-purpose flour

1 tbsp (14 g) mahleb

FOR THE CAKE

1½ cups (190 g) all-purpose flour

1 tsp mahleb

1 tsp baking powder

Pinch of salt

½ cup (120 g) unsalted butter, softened

¾ cup (150 g) superfine/caster sugar

4 egg yolks

½ cup plus 1 tbsp (135 ml) milk, room temperature

1 tsp vanilla extract

1⅓ cups (200 g) fresh or frozen morello cherries, pitted and halved

Mahleb is a fragrant spice made from the pits of wild cherries. It has a subtle marzipan flavor with sweet, fruity notes that complement the cherries. The sponge, made from just the yolks of the eggs, give the softest, most tender crumb, with the juice from the bursting cherries seeping into it. My favorite part is the crunchy texture that comes from the crumble topping, turning this into a hybrid of part-cake and part-dessert. It'll work equally as well with lashings of hot custard as it does on its own with a mug of tea.

YIELD: 8–10 SERVINGS

Preheat the oven to 350°F (180°C). Grease a deep, round 8-inch (20-cm) loose-bottomed cake pan and line with parchment paper.

To make the crumble topping, rub together the cold butter, sugar, flour and mahleb in a bowl with your fingertips to make a rough crumble. Put this in the fridge to firm up.

To make the cake, sift together the flour, mahleb, baking powder and salt in a medium bowl. Set aside. Using a stand mixer or electric whisk, beat the butter and sugar until pale and fluffy. Add the yolks one at a time, beating well after each addition and scraping down the sides of the bowl every so often. Stir in half of the flour mixture followed by the milk and vanilla. Fold in the rest of the flour. Spoon the batter into the prepared pan, spreading it out evenly. Top the batter evenly with the cherries. If you're using frozen cherries, there's no need to thaw. Finish with the chilled crumble. Bake for 40 to 50 minutes, or until a toothpick inserted in the center comes out clean. It may come out with some of the fruit juice and this is fine. Allow to cool completely in the pan before slicing and serving.

Tip: If you're unable to get ahold of mahleb at the store or online, you can substitute ¼ teaspoon of almond extract for every 1 teaspoon of mahleb. Almond extract is much more pungent, though, so be careful not to go overboard!

HIDDEN PEAR CAKE

3⅛ cups (750 ml) ginger beer

½ cup (100 g) granulated sugar

2 tsp (10 g) vanilla bean paste

2 cinnamon sticks

2 cardamom pods

3 small Conference or Bosc pears, peeled with stems intact

FOR THE CAKE

2 cups (250 g) all-purpose flour

2 tsp (10 g) baking powder

½ cup (115 g) unsalted butter

⅔ cup (150 g) light brown sugar

2 eggs

1 tsp molasses or treacle

½ cup (120 ml) milk

1 tsp vanilla extract

2 tbsp (30 g) finely chopped cryslalized ginger

The cross-section of this cake is simply stunning. Prepare yourself for the oohs and aahs that will ensue as you slice to reveal a perfectly poached pear sitting snug inside a warm, lightly spiced cake. The ripe-but-firm pears are completely the star of the show here.

YIELD: 6–8 SERVINGS

Preheat the oven to 325°F (170°C). Grease a 2-pound (900-g) loaf pan and line the bottom with parchment paper, leaving an overhang of 1 inch (2.5 cm) to help you lift the cake out when it's baked.

To make the poached pears, add the ginger beer, sugar, vanilla, cinnamon and cardamom to a large pot. Add the pears and simmer until they are tender enough for a fork to pierce them with a little force, 15 to 30 minutes, depending on how ripe the pears are. Remove the pears from the liquid and set aside.

To make the cake, sift together the flour and baking powder and set aside. Using a stand mixer, beat the butter and sugar for 2 to 3 minutes, or until pale and fluffy. Add the eggs one at a time, beating well after each addition. Stir in the molasses until smooth. With the mixer on low, pour in half of the flour followed by the milk and beat briefly to combine. Pour in the rest of the flour before adding the vanilla and ginger.

Pour the batter into the prepared pan. Slice the base off each pear to make sure it can sit upright without falling. Place the pears in the batter, gently pushing them in. Bake the cake for 15 minutes before opening the oven to gently straighten the pears if they have fallen. Bake for 50 to 65 minutes, or until a toothpick inserted into the center comes out clean. Let the cake cool for 30 minutes before lifting it from the pan to cool completely.

PEACH & ROSEMARY PAVLOVA

FOR THE MERINGUE
LAYERS

1¼ cups (250 g) superfine/caster sugar

Squeeze of lemon

²/₃ cup (150 g) egg whites

1 tsp cornstarch

To know me is to know that I love a good pavlova. If I'm having friends for dinner, two things are certain: there will always be at least two desserts on offer, and one of them will be a huge pavlova. This pavlova is majestic in its appearance with a crisp shell, marshmallow-like interior and bulging with fresh cream and a fruity filling. It is such a crowd-pleaser and as the meringue can be made in advance, all you need to do is fill it right before serving. This version gives off a peaches-and-cream vibe with a little update of fresh rosemary. Using herbs in cakes and desserts is such an easy way to give an unexpected twist that just works.

YIELD: 12–16 SERVINGS

Preheat the oven to 375°F (190°C). Line two baking trays with parchment paper. Use an 8-inch (20-cm) plate or cake pan to trace an outline with a pencil on both pieces of parchment. Turn the parchment upside down so the meringue won't come into contact with the pencil markings.

To make the meringue layers, add the sugar to a deep baking dish lined with parchment paper and heat in the oven for about 5 minutes. This makes it easier for the sugar to dissolve in the egg whites. Remove the sugar from the oven when the edges start to melt, and turn the temperature of the oven to 250°F (120°C).

Using a stand mixer with the whisk attachment, add the lemon juice and use a paper towel to wipe this around the entire bowl. This helps to eliminate any traces of grease that would prevent the meringue from whipping up. Add the egg whites and whip on low speed for 2 minutes before increasing the speed to medium-high to make the whites foamy. When the egg whites get to stiff peaks, and with the mixer still running, start adding the hot sugar, a spoonful at a time. Leave 10 to 15 seconds before adding in the next spoonful.

Once all the sugar has been added, whisk for 2 minutes, or until the meringue is thick, glossy and smooth. Add the cornstarch and whisk for a few seconds to combine. The meringue is ready when you can turn the bowl upside down with nothing falling out.

Using the circles you traced on the parchment paper as a guide, spoon the meringue onto both trays, carefully spreading it out to fill the circles. They don't need to look perfectly smooth as they'll be covered in cream. Bake in the cooled oven (250°F [120°C]) for 90 minutes, or until the meringues are firm to the touch and sound hollow when tapped. Leave them inside the oven with the door closed to cool completely for at least 2 hours, but preferably overnight.

(Continued)

PEACH & ROSEMARY PAVLOVA (CONTINUED)

2½ cups (400 g) fresh ripe or canned peaches

¼ cup (50 g) superfine/caster sugar

3 or more fresh rosemary sprigs

1 tbsp (15 ml) lemon juice

3 tbsp (45 ml) water

2½ cups (600 ml) heavy cream

1 tbsp (15 ml) vanilla extract

Scant ⅔ cup (100 g) shaved white chocolate

To make the filling, peel, core and thickly slice the peaches. Add them to a medium saucepan with the sugar, rosemary, lemon and water. Let the mixture simmer for 8 to 10 minutes, or until the peaches have softened. Let the peaches cool before removing the rosemary sprigs. I like to keep the filling quite chunky, but if you prefer, you can pulse the peaches in a food processor for a smoother texture.

To make the whipped cream, whip the heavy cream and vanilla in a bowl until you have stiff peaks. Be careful not to overwhip. Keep this in the fridge until you are ready to assemble.

To assemble the pavlova, take the first layer of meringue and place it on a large plate or serving board. Top it with half of the whipped cream followed by half of the white chocolate shavings. Add half of the peaches before placing the second meringue layer on top. Cover this layer with the remaining cream, remaining white chocolate shavings and the rest of the peaches. Garnish with a couple more rosemary sprigs.

Tip: Make this as one big meringue cake like I've done or you could bake individual ones. If that's how you choose to go, reduce the cooking time in half. The meringues, unfilled, will keep in an airtight container for 2 days.

POMEGRANATE MOLASSES CAKE WITH LABNEH ICING

FOR THE CAKE

³/₄ cup (175 g) unsalted butter

³/₄ cup plus 2 tbsp (175 g) superfine/caster sugar

3 eggs

2¹/₂ tbsp (38 ml) pomegranate molasses

Zest of 1 orange

1 tsp vanilla extract

1¹/₄ cups (150 g) all-purpose flour

¹/₂ tsp baking soda

¹/₂ tsp baking powder

Pinch of salt

¹/₄ cup (60 ml) buttermilk, at room temperature

FOR THE TOPPING

1¹/₂ cups (350 ml) labneh

2 tbsp (15 g) confectioners' sugar

1 tsp vanilla

Handful of fresh pomegranate seeds

The first time I came across pomegranate molasses, I was expecting it to be incredibly sweet and as bright in color as the jewel-like seeds. What I found instead was a deep, dark syrup with an intense sour flavor and a hint of sweetness. I was excited to experiment and explore how using molasses differed from fresh pomegranates. After throwing a few splashes into a cake batter, I was pleasantly surprised with the results: a sweet, sharp flavor that sat well with the creamy, strained yogurt topping.

YIELD: 8–10 SERVINGS

Preheat the oven to 350°F (180°C). Grease a deep, round 8-inch (20-cm) cake pan and line the bottom with parchment paper.

To make the cake, melt the butter and sugar in a medium saucepan, and then transfer to a large bowl to cool slightly. Beat in the eggs one at a time before stirring in the pomegranate molasses, orange zest and vanilla. Stir in the flour, baking soda, baking powder and salt until fully combined. Stir in the buttermilk before pouring into the prepared pan and baking for 30 to 40 minutes, or until a toothpick inserted in the center comes out clean. Leave to cool for 5 minutes before turning it out onto a wire rack to cool completely.

To make the topping, mix together the labneh, sugar and vanilla in a medium bowl until smooth. Spoon it generously on top of the cake and sprinkle with the pomegranate seeds.

*See photo on page 128.

Tip: Labneh is a Middle Eastern soft cream cheese made from strained yogurt. If you can't find it, you can make a substitute by adding Greek yogurt and a pinch of salt to a colander lined with muslin or a clean tea towel set over a bowl. Tie it up, secure with an elastic band and place it in the fridge for 12 to 24 hours before unwrapping and using.

PINEAPPLE & SAFFRON SYRUP CAKES

When I was a child, pineapples were the only fruit that I'd eat. You couldn't give me anything remotely fruity unless it was a pineapple. Everything about it was just perfect for me: the sweetness, the texture and especially the color. These little syrup cakes are bright and beautiful, soaked in a sweet saffron-scented syrup before being topped with caramelized pineapple.

YIELD: 12 CAKES

FOR THE CAKES

5 tbsp (75 ml) milk

Scant ½ cup (75 g) coarse polenta

⅔ cup (120 g) superfine/caster sugar, divided

½ cup (120 g) unsalted butter

1¼ cups (120 g) ground almonds

½ tsp baking powder

¼ tsp salt

2 eggs

1 tbsp (15 ml) pineapple juice

FOR THE SYRUP

Scant ⅔ cup (150 ml) pineapple juice

Squeeze of lime

¾ cup (150 g) superfine/caster sugar

4-5 saffron threads

FOR THE PINEAPPLE TOPPING

2½ cups (400 g) fresh ripe pineapple, chopped into small chunks

Squeeze of lime

¼ cup (50 g) granulated sugar

Preheat the oven to 350°F (180°C). Grease the holes of a 12-hole cupcake tray. Dust each one lightly with flour, tapping out the excess.

To make the cakes, add the milk, polenta and 1 tablespoon (15 g) of the sugar to a saucepan. Gently heat and stir constantly until the polenta has thickened and absorbed the milk. Set aside to cool. Using a stand mixer or electric whisk, beat the butter and remaining sugar for 3 to 5 minutes, or until pale and creamy. Mix in the almonds, baking powder and salt and beat for 1 minute, or until combined. Add the eggs one at a time, beating well after each addition and then mix in the polenta mix. Stir in the pineapple juice before dividing the batter evenly between the cupcake holes. Bake for 20 to 25 minutes, or until the cakes are firm around the edges and a toothpick inserted into the center comes out clean. Remove from the oven and leave them in the pan.

To make the syrup, heat the pineapple juice, lime, sugar and saffron threads in a small saucepan until the sugar has dissolved. Bring to a boil before removing from the heat. Spoon the syrup over the cakes, allowing it to sink inside. Let the cakes cool before removing from the pan and placing on a wire rack to cool completely.

To make the pineapple topping, place the pineapple on a baking tray and pat dry with a paper towel. Squeeze the lime on top and then sprinkle on the granulated sugar before using a blowtorch in a sweeping motion to caramelize the pineapple. Alternatively, you could place them under the grill or broiler for a few minutes. Add a few chunks onto each cake before drizzling with a little more syrup before serving.

BLUEBERRY, LEMON & LAVENDER FRANGIPANE

FOR THE CURD

2 eggs

³/₄ cup plus 2 tbsp (175 g) superfine/caster sugar

Zest and juice of 3 lemons

¹/₂ cup (115 g) unsalted butter, softened and diced

FOR THE FRANGIPANE

1 tsp dried lavender

1 cup (200 g) granulated sugar

³/₄ cup plus 2 tbsp (200 g) unsalted butter, softened

Zest of 1 lemon

3 eggs

2 cups (200 g) ground almonds

¹/₃ cup (40 g) all-purpose flour

20–30 fresh or frozen blueberries

Flaked almonds, for topping

Confectioners' sugar, to dust

When it comes to a classic frangipane tart, the frangipane layer is my favorite part. The thick, moist almond filling gets studded with various stone fruits and berries. I've stripped back the tart to just have the puffy, cake-like layer all on its own with a layer of zingy lemon curd hiding in the middle, scented with lavender and the juiciest blueberries nestling on top.

YIELD: 8–10 SERVINGS

Preheat the oven to 375°F (190°C). Grease the insides of six loose-bottomed, 4-inch (10-cm) tart cases with a little butter.

To make the curd, whisk the eggs in a medium bowl briefly to break them up. Whisk in the sugar, lemon zest and juice before transferring the mixture to a medium saucepan. Cook the curd on low heat, stirring constantly. Add the butter bit by bit while stirring and let it melt into the mixture. Cook the curd until it thickens enough to coat the back of a spoon. Pour into a bowl, cover and chill in the fridge.

To make the frangipane, add the lavender to a food processor and blend for 10 to 20 seconds to break it down. Pour in the sugar and pulse for 10 seconds, or until the lavender is ground with the sugar. Be careful not to process too much or you'll end up with powdered sugar.

Using a stand mixer or electric whisk, beat the butter, lavender/sugar mix and lemon zest for 3 to 5 minutes, or until pale and creamy. Add the eggs one at a time, beating well after each addition. Stir in the almonds and flour and beat until combined. Transfer the batter to a large disposable piping bag and snip off about a ¹/₂ inch (1.3 cm) from the end. Pipe a thin layer onto the base of each tart case and then add about 1 teaspoon of lemon curd on top. Smooth this with the back of a teaspoon to even it out before piping on another layer of the frangipane, filling each case about three-quarters full. Top each cake with 4 to 6 blueberries, depending on their size, and sprinkle with a few flaked almonds. Bake for 15 to 20 minutes, or until the frangipanes are golden brown. Place them on a wire rack to cool completely in their cases before dusting with confectioners' sugar and serving.

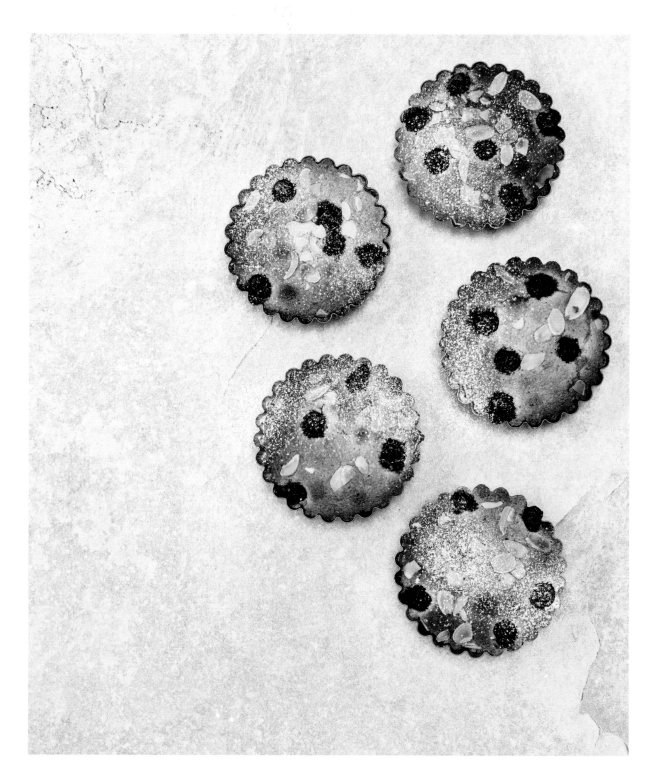

RHUBARB, ROSE & ALMOND CAKE

¾ cup (170 g) unsalted butter

1 cup (200 g) superfine/caster sugar

½ tsp rosewater

Zest of 1 lemon

2 eggs

1⅓ cups (175 g) all-purpose flour

¾ cup (80 g) ground almonds

1 tsp baking powder

½ tsp baking soda

½ cup (120 ml) plain yogurt

½ lb (200–250 g) rhubarb, washed

1 tbsp (15 g) granulated or demerara sugar, for topping

Confectioners' sugar, to dust

It's the bright pink candy hues of forced rhubarb that entices me to this cake. With such a mesmerizing natural color, it needed to be used in a cake that would let it peek through the sponge and not get buried underneath. Although the appearance of rhubarb might tell your brain that it's going to be tooth-achingly sweet, the opposite is true. Uncooked, forced rhubarb is incredibly tart and sour but sweetens as it cooks, making it great for cakes and other desserts. Fragranced with a little rosewater to balance it out, this is a fitting cake to celebrate the seasonal arrival of one of the prettiest vegetables around.

YIELD: 8 SERVINGS

Preheat the oven to 325°F (170°C). Grease a round, loose-bottomed 9-inch (23-cm) cake pan and line the bottom with parchment paper.

Using a stand mixer or electric whisk, beat the butter, sugar and rosewater for 3 to 5 minutes, or until pale and fluffy. Stir in the lemon zest, and then add the eggs one at a time, beating well after each addition. Add the flour, almonds, baking powder and baking soda and mix on low speed until just combined. Stir in the yogurt by hand before transferring the batter into the prepared pan and smoothing the top.

Cut the rhubarb into strips that are approximately 3 to 4 inches (7 to 10 cm) long and arrange them on top of the batter in a radial pattern, letting them overlap each other. Sprinkle on the granulated sugar and bake for 50 to 60 minutes, or until the cake is a deep golden brown and a toothpick inserted into the center comes out free from cake batter. Let the cake cool completely before dusting with confectioners' sugar.

Tips: Different brands of rosewater vary tremendously in strength, so start with ½ teaspoon in the recipe and add more to taste. Using forced rhubarb has the benefit of that wonderful pink color, but when out of season, regular rhubarb works just as well.

DATE & ROOIBOS LOAF

Scant 1 cup (240 ml) boiling water

2 rooibos tea bags

1 cup (140 g) pitted and roughly chopped dates

1 tsp baking soda

⅓ cup (75 g) unsalted butter

1¾ cups (225 g) all-purpose flour

¼ tsp salt

½ cup plus 1 tbsp (125 g) light muscovado sugar

2 tsp (10 g) baking powder

½ tsp ground cinnamon

1 egg

1 tsp vanilla bean paste

As I've gotten older, my love for dates has grown, and I've come to enjoy their natural sweetness and versatility in both sweet and savory dishes as well as their ability to be kept and used all year-round, unlike fresh fruits. Here, they not only keep the cake incredibly moist but also complement the earthy flavor of the rooibos. I love baking with tea, as it's such an easy way to add an aromatic element to your cakes with minimal effort. Don't skimp on the steeping time for the tea, though, as this will help get the most flavor. A slice of this loaf is best served lightly toasted with a good lashing of salted butter . . . the perfect afternoon treat.

YIELD: SERVES 6–8

Preheat the oven to 350°F (180°C). Grease a 2-pound (900-g) loaf pan and line with parchment paper.

Pour the boiling water into a bowl, add the tea bags and steep for 5 minutes. Place the dates in a large bowl, pour in the tea and discard the tea bags. Stir in the baking soda and butter until fully melted, and leave the dates to soften in the liquid for 10 minutes.

In a medium bowl, sift together the flour, salt, sugar, baking powder and cinnamon. Set aside.

Once the dates have softened, whisk in the egg and then stir in the vanilla and dry ingredients, making sure you don't have any lumps of flour hiding at the bottom. Pour into the prepared pan and bake for 40 to 45 minutes, or until a toothpick inserted comes out clean without any traces of batter. Allow the cake to cool for 10 minutes in the pan before turning it out onto a wire rack to cool completely. Serve with a good spread of butter.

Tip: I've used Medjool dates here, simply because of the beautiful caramel-like flavor, which lets the delicate tea notes shine. You can of course use Deglet Noor dates, which are inexpensive and easy to get ahold of—just be aware that these aren't as sweet as Medjool and so you may wish to adjust the sugar quantities slightly.

SUMMER BERRY CAKE

A feather-light genoise sponge sits underneath a cloud of creamy vanilla mascarpone and is piled with the very best fruits that summer has to offer. I'm certain that this cake would be gladly received at any barbecue or picnic, and whenever I make it, it disappears within minutes. The genoise can be a little tricky to master, as all the rise in the cake comes from whipping the eggs—there's no additional leavening, so it's important to be gentle when folding in the flour to get the airiest sponge possible.

YIELD: 1 ROUND 8-INCH (20-CM) CAKE

FOR THE SPONGE

4 eggs

1 egg yolk

²/₃ cup (130 g) superfine/caster sugar

1 cup (125 g) all-purpose flour

2 tbsp (30 g) unsalted butter, melted

FOR THE SYRUP

½ cup (100 g) superfine/caster sugar

⅓ cup (80 ml) water

1 tsp vanilla bean paste

FOR THE CREAM

1 cup (225 g) mascarpone

½ cup (65 g) confectioners' sugar

1 tsp vanilla extract

½ cup (120 ml) heavy cream

Zest of 1 lemon

FOR ASSEMBLY

Approximately ¼–½ cup (35–75 g) each of raspberries, blueberries, blackberries, strawberries and cherries

Handful of flaked almonds, for topping

Tip: This cake has the ability to look completely different every time you make it. Choose your favorite berries or summer fruits and pile them on like I've done for a more rustic finish or arrange them in a wreath for something more organized.

Preheat the oven to 350°F (180°C). Grease a round 8-inch (20-cm) cake pan and line with parchment paper.

To make the sponge, add the eggs, egg yolk and sugar to the bowl of a stand mixer or heatproof bowl and set it over a pan of simmering water. Make sure the bottom of the bowl doesn't touch the water. Whisk the eggs until the sugar has dissolved and the mixture is warm to the touch. Remove the bowl from the heat and continue to whisk the eggs with a stand mixer fitted with the whisk attachment or an electric whisk. It will take approximately 4 to 7 minutes for the eggs to be thick, pale and tripled in volume. To test that the eggs are ready and have reached ribbon stage, turn off the mixer, lift out the whisk and let the mixture fall back in. It should leave a trail on the surface that will sink and disappear after a few seconds. If this doesn't happen, continue to whisk and repeat.

Sift one-third of the flour on top of the eggs and very gently fold it in. You want to be careful not to knock out all of the air you've just incorporated. Sift in the remaining flour and fold, making sure there are no pockets of flour hiding toward the bottom of the bowl. Carefully take out approximately ½ cup (120 ml) (doesn't need to be exact) of the batter and put it in a small bowl. Pour in the melted butter and stir to thoroughly combine. Fold the butter mixture back into the batter. Gently pour the batter into the prepared cake pan and bake for 35 to 45 minutes. If the cake looks like it's getting too brown, loosely cover it with a sheet of foil. Leave the cake to cool in the pan for 5 minutes before turning it out onto a wire rack to cool completely.

To make the syrup, bring the sugar, water and vanilla to a rolling boil in a saucepan, stirring regularly to dissolve the sugar. Set aside to cool.

To make the cream, place the mascarpone, sugar and vanilla in a medium bowl and beat with a wooden spoon or spatula until smooth. In a small bowl, whisk the cream to get soft peaks and then fold this into the mascarpone. Stir in the lemon zest and set aside until you're ready to assemble. Once the cake has cooled, poke holes across the top with a toothpick and pour the syrup all over. Spread the mascarpone on top (you can cover the sides, too, if you prefer) and then decorate with the fresh berries and almonds.

ACKNOWLEDGMENTS

Although my name appears on the front cover, this book is the result of so many more people behind the scenes.

A huge thank you to my family, who put up with my constant chaos and mess in the kitchen while I tested all the recipes and took over the entire fridge. Thank you to the one and only Mama Bo, who washed up for me when I was too tired, used her magical skills to keep the cupboards organized, helped with all the (very many) supermarket runs and for just being so encouraging. Thank you to Nathan who told me every cake was a 10 out of 10 and to Bonita who told me when they weren't.

I have to thank the family at BLoC for their support, prayers, constant checking in to make sure I was doing okay and for taking my mind off book stuff through countless Sunday roasts.

While I had an idea in my head of what I wanted my first book to look like, it was brought to life by the incredibly talented Holly Wulff Petersen, who photographed everything in this book. There was no one else I wanted to work with on this, so thank you for saying yes and capturing such beautiful images.

Shooting the recipes was such a fun process, but it wouldn't have gone as smoothly as it did without my incredible assistants! Thank you to Georgie and Lola for all your amazing help in the kitchen.

A big thank you to the team at Northbank Talent Management. To Martin, for your patience in getting this all going, and to James, for being such a great agent during the years.

Last, thank you to my publishers and editors at Page Street, who reached out about writing a book and both understood and developed my vision. Thank you for allowing me to express myself in this way and for letting my voice shine through.

ABOUT THE AUTHOR

Benjamina Ebuehi is a London-based baker and food stylist who finished as a quarter finalist on *The Great British Bake Off* in 2016. Since the show, she has gone on to develop recipes and content for brands, host workshops and classes, launch The Sister Table (a series of award-winning pop-up brunch clubs for women) and be an ambassador for the social enterprise Luminary Bakery.

INDEX